Quilted
Bags & Gifts

Quilted Bags & Gifts
Published in 2016 by Zakka Workshop, a division of World Book Media LLC

www.zakkaworkshop.com
134 Federal Street
Salem, MA 01970 USA
info@zakkaworkshop.com

Copyright © 2015 Akemi Shibata
SHIBATA AKEMI SEKAI DE TATTA HITOTSU ANATA DAKE NO PATCHWORK
Originally published in Japanese language by Boutique-sha, Tokyo, Japan
English language rights, translation & production by Zakka Workshop
Japanese Editors: Hisako Arai and Yoko Sanjo
English Editors: Lindsay Fair, Maureen Clark and Kristyne Czepuryk
Translation: Kyoko Matthews

ISBN: 978-1-940552-23-1

Printed in China
10 9 8 7 6 5 4 3 2 1

Quilted
Bags & Gifts

36 Classic Quilting Projects to Make and Give

Akemi Shibata

Introduction

My husband's family owns a craft store. When I first joined the family, I was excited to work in the shop because I've always loved sewing and knitting. Unfortunately, I felt useless and out of place compared to the talented and experienced staff.

However, everything changed when I first encountered the art of quilting. I fell in love with this new and colorful world. In fact, I would lose track of time and stay up all night sewing. Quilting has become one of the greatest joys in my life.

No matter how busy my schedule becomes, I set aside time for quilting each and every day because it keeps me sane. I know that I will keep on quilting until I can't see or hold a needle anymore! I love teaching and holding workshops because it provides an opportunity to share the joy of quilting with others. I hope the projects in this book inspire the same feeling within you!

AKEMI SHIBATA

Contents

Before You Begin 6

Projects

1. Hexagon Flower Tote 14

2. City Life Tote. 17

3. Dancing Tulips Bucket Bag 20

4. Appliquéd Tulip Purse. 25

5. Two-Way Hexagon Purse 30

6. Cross-Body Bouquet Bag 34

7. Newsprint Backpack 37

8. Swivel Hook Tote. 42

9. Classic Bowling Bag 45

10. Home Sweet Home Tote 48

11. Home Sweet Home Pouch. 48

12. Irish Chain Tote 54

13. Modern Quilter's Bag 57

14. Double Wedding Ring Tote. . . . 60

15. Embellished Patch Tote 63

16. Appliquéd Boston Bag 66

17. Embroidered Eyeglass Case. . . . 66

18. Hawaiian Carryall 74

19. Village Tablet Case. 78

20. House Pencil Case. 78

21. Bluebird Basket. 84

22. Bluebird Tea Mat 84

23. Hexagon Coin Purse 88

24. Hexagon Zip Pouch. 88

25. Tea Time Pouch 93

26. Owl Coin Purse 93

27. Appliquéd Sewing Box 98

28. Floral Scissor Caddy. 99

29. Elephant Tape Measure Case . 99

30. Flower Pin Cushion 99

31. Floral Basket 108

32. Floral Coasters. 108

33. Pastoral Wall Hanging 111

34. Countryside Collage 111

35. Quilt As You Go Sampler. 114

36. Quilt Block Totes. 115

Templates 121

Before You Begin

Before you get started on the projects, here are a few basic techniques to review. I've also included some of my personal tips, so even if you're an experienced quilter, you might learn something new!

PATCHWORK

How to Make Templates

Photocopy or trace the templates printed in the book or on the pattern sheet. You can use paper templates or create more durable ones from card stock. To do this, tape the photocopy to a piece of card stock. Mark the corners by using a stiletto to punch holes in the card stock. Connect the marks, then cut out the card stock template.

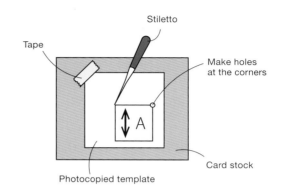

How to Cut Your Pieces Out of Fabric

Align your fabric on your work surface with the wrong side facing up. Trace around your template. Make sure to leave space between each piece when tracing multiple templates. Use a ruler to draw ¼" (0.7 cm) seam allowance around each piece. Cut the pieces out along the seam allowance line.

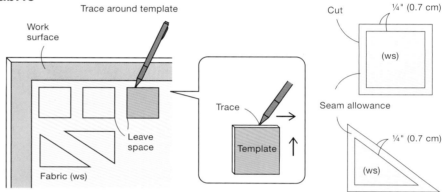

How to Hand Piece

Getting Set Up

Thread a needle with one strand of neutral-colored thread. Your thread should measure about 11 ¾" (30 cm) long. Tie a knot at the end of the thread. You may want to wear a leather thimble on your middle finger to push the needle as you sew.

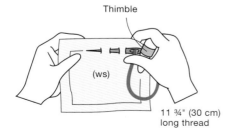

How to Sew Pieces Together from Edge to Edge

1. Align two pieces of fabric with right sides together. Insert a pin at each seam allowance (① and ②), then as many more as necessary to hold the two pieces of fabric together (③). Working from right to left, insert your needle at ① and make one backstitch in the seam allowance. Running stitch to ②. Finger press the seam to smooth out wrinkles. Make one backstitch in the seam allowance, then make a knot. Press the seam allowance toward the darker fabric.

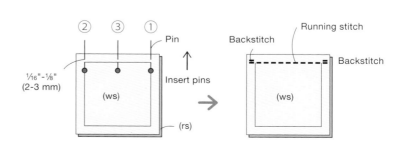

2. To sew the two sets together, align the center seams. Sew together following the same process used in step 1, but make one backstitch at the center seam. Press the seam allowance to one side.

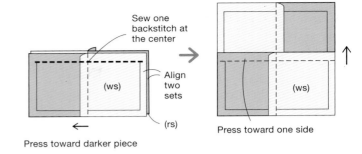

How to Sew Inset Seams

For certain shapes, such as hexagons and diamonds, you'll need to sew the pieces together using inset seams.

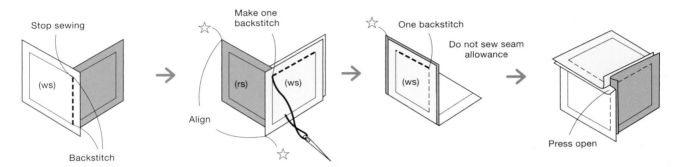

1. Sew the first two pieces together starting and stopping at the seam allowance.

2. Attach the next piece using the same process. Make one backstitch when you reach the seam allowance. Do not cut the thread. Align the ☆s.

3. Insert the needle through the fabric, avoiding the seam allowance. Sew along the remaining side. Make one backstitch when you reach the seam allowance. Make a knot.

4. Press the seam allowance open.

APPLIQUÉ

Note: You may want to cut your appliqué pieces out with a slightly smaller seam allowance than your patchwork pieces. I recommend using a ¼" (0.5 cm) seam allowance.

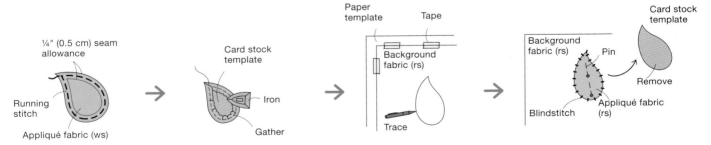

1. Running stitch in the seam allowance of the appliqué piece, leaving long thread tails.

2. Align the card stock template on the wrong side of the appliqué piece. Pull the thread tails to gather the seam allowance around the template. Iron to set the shape of the appliqué piece.

3. Use the paper template to trace the appliqué motif onto the right side of the background fabric. You may need to use a lightbox.

4. Remove the card stock template and blindstitch the appliqué piece to the background fabric. When blindstitching, try to stitch through the folded seam allowance of the appliqué piece.

QUILTING

How to Mark Your Quilting Lines

Mark quilting lines on the right side of your quilt top using a sharply pointed fabric pencil. Draw quickly and dust off extra lead powder as you work in order to keep the quilt top clean. I recommend a gridded ruler when drawing diagonal quilting lines. Always start from the center and work outward.

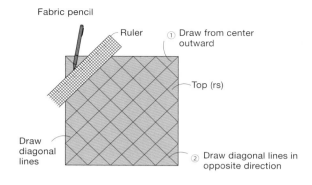

Fabric pencil

Ruler

① Draw from center outward

Top (rs)

Draw diagonal lines

② Draw diagonal lines in opposite direction

How to Baste

Working on a flat surface, layer the top, batting, and backing. Pin the layers together. Use one strand of basting thread to make basting stitches ⅝" (1.5 cm) apart. Use a plastic spoon to receive the needle as you stitch. This will keep your fingers from getting sore. Start from the center of the quilt and work outward, sewing seams ①–④ in numerical order. Each basting seam should be 2"-2 ½" (5-6 cm) apart. Finally, baste around the outer edge of the quilt.

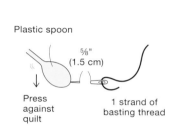

Plastic spoon

⅝" (1.5 cm)

Press against quilt

1 strand of basting thread

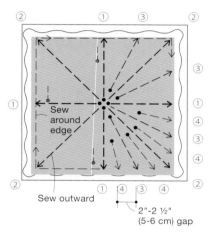

Sew around edge

Sew outward

2"-2 ½" (5-6 cm) gap

How to Hand Quilt

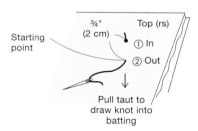

Starting point

¾" (2 cm)

Top (rs)

① In

② Out

Pull taut to draw knot into batting

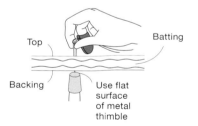

Top

Batting

Backing

Use flat surface of metal thimble

Leather thimble

Use corner of metal thimble

1. Thread your needle with one strand of quilting thread. I usually use a neutral color, such as beige, white, or gray. Make a knot at the end of the thread. Insert your needle through the right side of the quilt top about ¾" (2 cm) away from the starting point. Draw the needle out on the right side at the starting point. Pull the thread taut to draw the knot through the quilt top so it is hidden in the batting.

2. Wear a leather thimble on the middle finger of your sewing hand and a metal thimble on the middle finger of your receiving hand. Push the needle through all three layers using the leather thimble. Receive the needle using the flat surface of the metal thimble.

3. Use the corner of the metal thimble to push the needle tip back up through all three layers.

Repeat steps 2 and 3

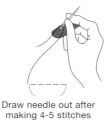

Draw needle out after making 4-5 stitches

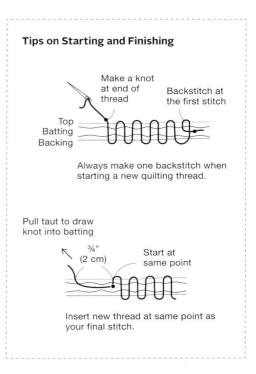

Tips on Starting and Finishing

Make a knot at end of thread

Backstitch at the first stitch

Top
Batting
Backing

Always make one backstitch when starting a new quilting thread.

Pull taut to draw knot into batting

¾"
(2 cm)

Start at same point

Insert new thread at same point as your final stitch.

4. Repeat steps 2 and 3 to make 4-5 stitches that are even in length and spaced 1⁄16" (1-2 mm) apart.

Note: Your stitches should be made with a rocking motion.

5. Draw the needle out and pull the stitches taut. Continue quilting until you reach the end of your thread. To finish a thread, make a knot on the right side of the quilt, then pull the thread taut to draw the knot through the quilt top so it becomes hidden in the batting. Cut the thread. Once the quilting is complete, remove the basting stitches.

How to Quilt Small Projects

When quilting a small project, gather the fabric between your hands. Pull the fabric taut in the area where you'll be working. Quilt, working toward yourself.

Note: The layers can shift easily when using this method, so make sure to baste before quilting.

Gather

Gather

Top

Quilt toward yourself

How to Quilt Large Projects

For large projects, such as bags and quilts, use a hoop to quilt small sections at a time. Set the fabric into the hoop loosely so that the fabric has a little give to it. Use your body to push the hoop against the edge of your table or desk. Use thimbles to quilt the area inside the hoop. Always work toward yourself when quilting.

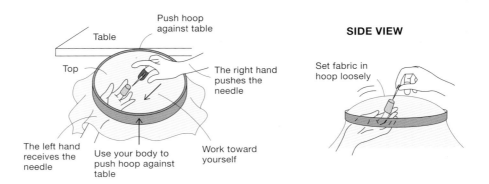

Push hoop against table

Table

Top

The right hand pushes the needle

The left hand receives the needle

Use your body to push hoop against table

Work toward yourself

SIDE VIEW

Set fabric in hoop loosely

BINDING

How to Prepare Bias Tape

Mark your fabric with 45° parallel lines 1 ½" (3.5 cm) apart and cut into strips. Align two bias strips with right sides together and sew using ¼" (0.7 cm) seam allowance. Continue sewing strips together until bias tape reaches the desired length.

Note: This book uses ⅜" (0.8 cm) finished binding for the majority of projects. This means that you'll need to cut 1 ½" (3.5 cm) wide binding strips (this measurement includes seam allowance). The individual project instructions will specify whether the strips should be cut lengthwise or on the bias.

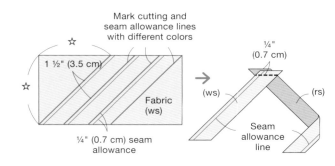

Mark cutting and seam allowance lines with different colors

1 ½" (3.5 cm)

Fabric (ws)

¼" (0.7 cm) seam allowance

¼" (0.7 cm)

(ws) (rs)

Seam allowance line

☆ = Equal distance

How to Bind the Quilt

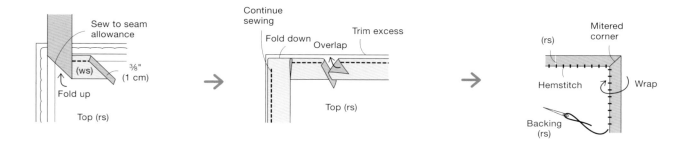

Sew to seam allowance

(ws)

⅜" (1 cm)

Fold up

Top (rs)

Continue sewing

Fold down

Overlap

Trim excess

Top (rs)

Mitered corner

(rs)

Hemstitch

Wrap

Backing (rs)

1. Fold the short end of the binding tape over ⅜" (1 cm). With right sides together, align the binding tape with the quilt, starting a short distance away from the corner. Sew the binding tape to the quilt, stopping when you reach the corner seam allowance. Fold the binding tape up and away from the quilt at a 45° angle.

2. Crease, then fold the binding strip back down, making a horizontal fold that aligns with the raw edge of the quilt. Continue sewing to attach the rest of the bias tape to the quilt, mitering each corner. When you reach the end, overlap the two short ends of the bias tape and sew until you are back at the starting point. Trim the excess seam allowance.

3. Wrap the binding around the seam allowance and hemstitch to the backing.

FINISHING TECHNIQUES

How to Assemble a Project Using the Whipstitch

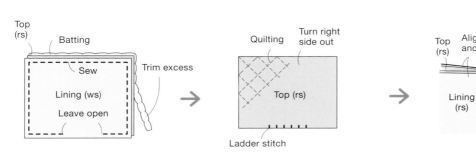

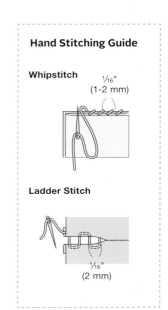

1. Layer the top and batting. Align the lining and top with right sides together. Sew along the edges, leaving an opening. Trim the batting seam allowances, then turn right side out through the opening.

2. Ladder stitch the opening closed. Quilt as desired. The bag front is now complete.

3. Repeat steps 1 and 2 to make the bag back. Align the quilted front and back with right sides together. Using a fine whipstitch, sew the pieces together, taking care to stitch through the top fabric only (do not stitch through the lining fabric).

How to Finish Seam Allowances Using the Lining

Note: This method requires one piece to have extra lining fabric to cover and finish the seam allowance. This extra fabric has already been added to the applicable pieces in the cutting instructions.

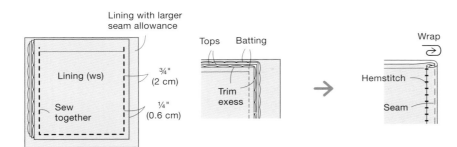

1. Align quilted front and back with right sides together. (**Note:** One lining has the extra fabric.) Sew the pieces together using a ¾" (2 cm) seam allowance that is based on the larger lining. Leave the larger seam allowance at ¾" (2 cm) and trim the other allowances to ¼" (0.6 cm).

2. Wrap the larger seam allowance around the others. Tuck the raw edge of the extra fabric underneath and hemstitch in place.

How to Hand Sew Zippers

1. Working from the wrong side, align one side of the zipper with bag lining and pin in place. The zipper teeth should start ⅛"-¼" (0.3-0.5 cm) in from the seam allowance.

2. Fold the short edges of the zipper as shown in the above diagram. Backstitch the zipper to the bag, making sure to stitch through the lining only so stitches aren't visible on the outside. Hemstitch the raw edge of the zipper to the lining. Repeat process to attach the other side of the zipper to the bag.

How to Make Covered Buttons

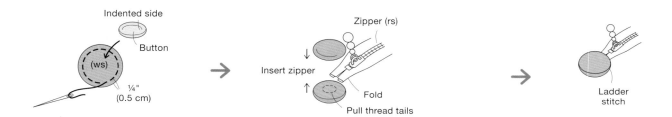

1. Running stitch around the circular fabric scrap using a ¼" (0.5 cm) seam allowance. Leave long thread tails. Center the button on the wrong side of the fabric so the indented side of the button faces up.

2. Pull the thread tails to gather the fabric around the button. Repeat process to make another covered button. Fold the raw edges of the zipper in half above the zipper stop. Sandwich the zipper end between two covered buttons.

3. Ladder stitch the two covered buttons together (refer to page 11).

How to Make Zipper Charms

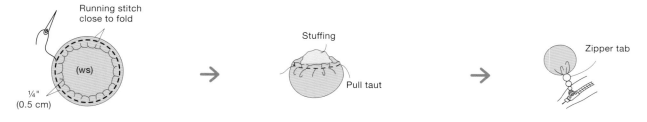

1. Fold the ¼" (0.5 cm) seam allowance to the wrong side of the circular fabric scrap. Running stitch the seam allowance, stitching as close to the fold as possible. Leave long thread tails.

2. Insert a bit of stuffing. Pull the thread tails taut to gather the fabric into a ball.

3. Insert the zipper tab into the stuffing and pull the thread tails taut. Secure the thread tails with a knot.

EMBROIDERY GUIDE

Most of the embroidery in this book is done with No. 25 embroidery floss. The individual project instructions will specify how many strands of floss should be used. If the project calls for No. 5 pearl cotton or candlewicking floss, use one strand.

RUNNING STITCH

FEATHER STITCH

LAZY DAISY STITCH

OUTLINE STITCH

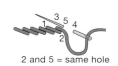

2 and 5 = same hole

FRENCH KNOT

SATIN STITCH

BACKSTITCH

COLONIAL KNOT

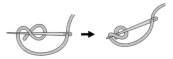

STRAIGHT STITCH

CHAIN STITCH

FLY STITCH

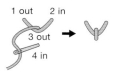

CROSS-STITCH

BLANKET STITCH

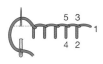

HERRINGBONE STITCH

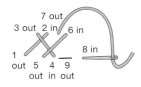

COUCHING STITCH

Hexagon Flower Tote

Hexagons are one of my favorite quilting motifs. In fact, I love English paper piecing hexagons so much, that I often forget to stop and eat lunch while in the midst of sewing these cute little shapes together. This floral inspired bag adds cheer to any outfit. Try changing the color scheme of the flowers for an entirely different look.

MATERIALS

- **Patchwork fabric:** Assorted scraps
- **Main fabric:** ⅝ yard of white print fabric
- **Lining fabric:** ⅝ yard of print fabric
- **Batting:** 19 ¾" x 39 ½" (50 x 100 cm)
- One set of 25" (63 cm) handles

PATCHWORK DIAGRAM

FRONT

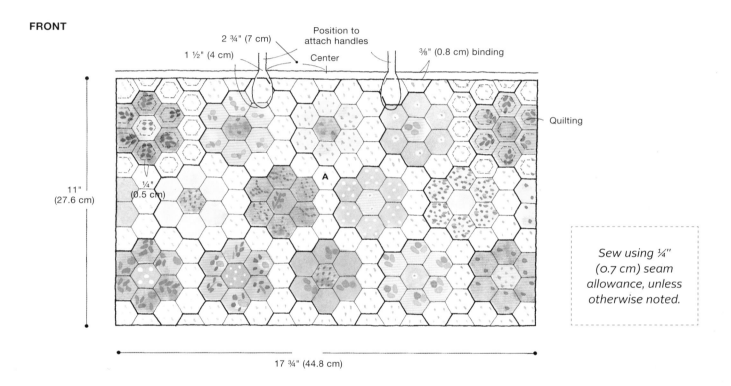

2 ¾" (7 cm)

1 ½" (4 cm)

Position to
attach handles

Center

⅜" (0.8 cm) binding

Quilting

11"
(27.6 cm)

¼"
(0.5 cm)

A

17 ¾" (44.8 cm)

*Sew using ¼"
(0.7 cm) seam
allowance, unless
otherwise noted.*

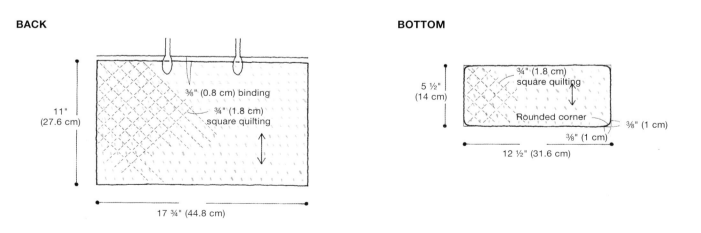

BACK

⅜" (0.8 cm) binding

¾" (1.8 cm)
square quilting

11"
(27.6 cm)

17 ¾" (44.8 cm)

BOTTOM

¾" (1.8 cm)
square quilting

Rounded corner

⅜" (1 cm)

5 ½"
(14 cm)

⅜" (1 cm)

12 ½" (31.6 cm)

CUTTING INSTRUCTIONS

Trace and cut out the template on page 121 (refer to page 6 for instructions on using templates). Cut the following fabric pieces adding ¼" (0.7 cm) seam allowance:

- 102 **A** pieces of assorted scraps (for flowers)
- 97 **A** pieces of main fabric (for background)

Cut out the following pieces, which do not have templates, according to the measurements on the right (these measurements include seam allowance):

Lining fabric:
- Front lining: 12" x 18 ¼" (30.3 x 46.2 cm)
- Back lining: 12" x 19 ¼" (30.3 x 48.8 cm)
- Bottom lining: 6" x 13" (15.4 x 33 cm)

Main fabric:
- Back: 11 ½" x 18 ¼" (29 x 46.2 cm)
- Bottom: 6" x 13" (15.4 x 33 cm)
- Binding strips (cut lengthwise): 1 ¼ yards (1.25 m) of 1 ½" (3.5 cm) wide strips

CONSTRUCTION STEPS

1. Use the English paper piecing technique shown in the diagram on page 89 to sew the hexagons into flower shapes. Sew the flower shapes together to create the bag front as shown in the diagram on page 15.

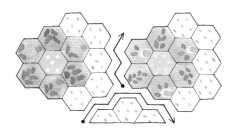

2. Layer the front, batting and lining. Quilt each hexagon as shown in the diagram on page 15. Next, layer the back, batting, and lining. Quilt as shown in the diagram on page 15. Use the technique shown on page 11 to sew the front and back together along the sides and finish the seam allowance using the lining.

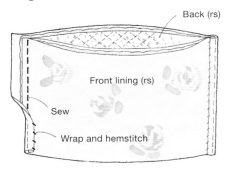

3. Layer the bottom, batting, and lining. Quilt with ¾" (1.8 cm) squares. Mark each side ⅜" (1 cm) from the corner. Connect the marks to make rounded corners. Use the technique shown on page 11 to sew the bottom to the bag and finish the seam allowance using the lining.

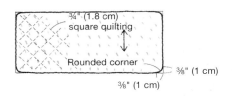

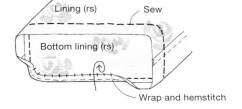

4. Use the binding strips to bind the bag opening. Backstitch the handles to the bag using two strands of quilting thread (refer to the diagram on page 15 for placement).

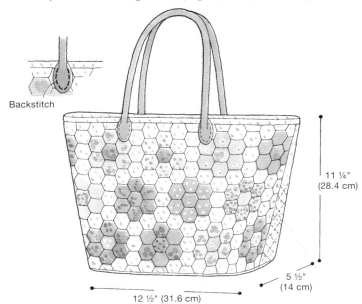

(2) City Life Tote

The geometric design of this bag may look complicated, but it's actually quite simple to construct. Try to incorporate a mix of stripes, dots, and text when choosing your fabrics—I love the way the different prints interact to make a graphic statement. The coordinating faux leather handles and trim lend this tote a very chic and modern look.

- **Light blue fabric:** ½ yard of light blue print fabric
- **White fabric:** ½ yard of white polka dot fabric
- **Striped fabric:** ⅝ yard of white striped fabric
- **Text fabric:** ½ yard of black and white text print fabric
- **Lining fabric:** ⅝ yard of print fabric
- **Batting:** 19 ¾" x 43 ¼" (50 x 110 cm)
- One set of 25" (63 cm) handles
- 39 ½" (100 cm) of ¾" (2 cm) wide faux leather tape

PATCHWORK DIAGRAM

FRONT

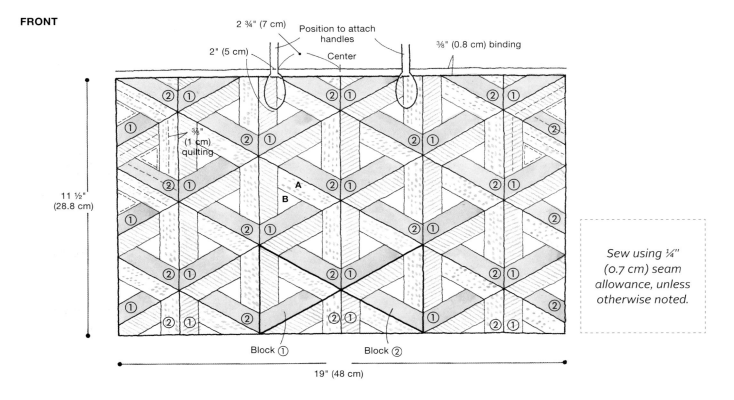

2 ¾" (7 cm)
Position to attach handles
2" (5 cm)
Center
⅜" (0.8 cm) binding
⅜" (1 cm) quilting
A
B
11 ½" (28.8 cm)
Block ①
Block ②
19" (48 cm)

Sew using ¼" (0.7 cm) seam allowance, unless otherwise noted.

BACK

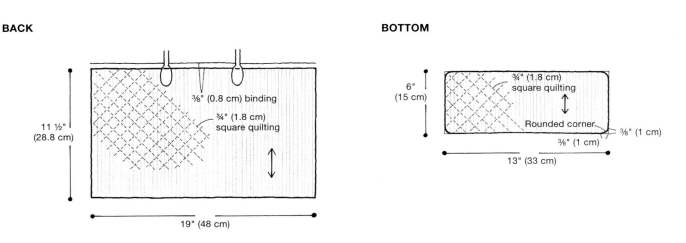

⅜" (0.8 cm) binding
¾" (1.8 cm) square quilting
11 ½" (28.8 cm)
19" (48 cm)

BOTTOM

¾" (1.8 cm) square quilting
6" (15 cm)
Rounded corner
⅜" (1 cm)
⅜" (1 cm)
13" (33 cm)

CUTTING INSTRUCTIONS

Trace and cut out the templates on page 121 (refer to page 6 for instructions on using templates). Cut the following fabric pieces adding ¼" (0.7 cm) seam allowance:

- 36 **A** pieces of light blue fabric
- 36 **B** pieces of white polka dot fabric
- 36 **A** pieces of striped fabric (cut on the bias)
- 36 **A** pieces of text fabric (cut on the bias)

Cut out the following pieces, which do not have templates, according to the measurements on the right (these measurements include seam allowance):

Lining fabric:
- Front lining: 12 ½" x 19 ½" (31.5 x 49.4 cm)
- Back lining: 12 ½" x 20 ½" (31.5 x 52 cm)
- Bottom lining: 6 ½" x 13 ½" (16.4 x 34.4 cm)

Striped fabric:
- Back: 12" x 19 ½" (30.2 x 49.4 cm)
- Bottom: 6 ½" x 13 ½" (16.4 x 34.4 cm)
- Binding strips (cut lengthwise): 1 ¼ yards (1.25 m) of 1 ½" (3.5 cm) wide strips

CONSTRUCTION STEPS

1. Make 21 each of Block ① and ② as shown below. Make six columns with seven blocks each, then sew the columns together to create the front (refer to diagram on page 18 for layout). Trim the front into a 12" x 19 ½" (30.2 x 49.4 cm) rectangle. Layer the front, batting, and lining. Quilt as shown in the diagram on page 18. Next, layer the back, batting, and backing. Quilt as shown in the diagram on page 18. Follow steps 2-4 on page 16 to sew the bag together and bind the bag opening.

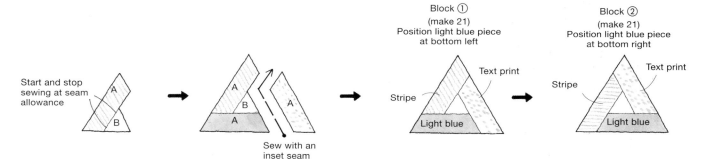

2. Align the faux leather tape with the binding so that the end of the tape matches up with the side seam of the bag. Backstitch one long edge of the tape to the binding on the outside of the bag. Fold the tape and hemstitch the other long edge to the binding on the inside of the bag.

3. Backstitch the handles to the bag using two strands of quilting thread (refer to the diagram on page 18 for placement).

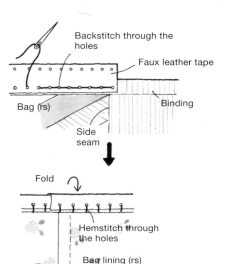

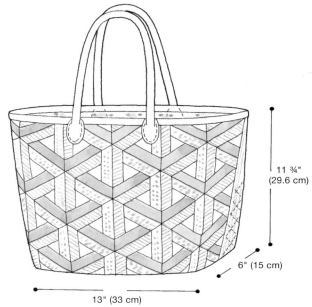

(3) Dancing Tulips Bucket Bag

This bag is so lovely that I am tempted to keep it for a display rather than use it! After much trial and error, I finally developed a technique for creating these majestic three-dimensional tulips and I couldn't be happier with the results.

MATERIALS

- **Appliqué fabric:** Assorted scraps
- **Fabric A:** ½ yard of beige polka dot fabric
- **Fabric B:** ⅝ yard of dark brown fabric
- **Fabric C:** ¼ yard of beige striped fabric
- **Fabric D:** ½ yard of light blue print fabric
- **Lining fabric:** ½ yard of print fabric
- **Batting:** 19 ¾" x 27 ½" (50 x 70 cm)
- Linen embroidery thread in beige
- Scraps of yarn

PATCHWORK DIAGRAM

FRONT & BACK

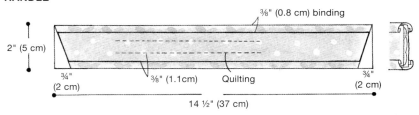

2 ¼" (5.5 cm) Position to attach handles
Center
⅜" (0.8 cm) binding
1 ¾" (4.5 cm)
⅝ " (1.5 cm)
Fabric A
Fabric B
Fly stitch (beige, 1 strand)
Fabric C
Appliqué
10 ½" (26.5 cm)
4" (10 cm)
¾" (2 cm) square quilting
3 ½" (9 cm)
Fabric D
2" (5 cm)
½" (1.3 cm)
½" (1.3 cm)
13" (33 cm)

HANDLE

⅜" (0.8 cm) binding
2" (5 cm)
¾" (2 cm)
⅜" (1.1cm) Quilting
¾" (2 cm)
14 ½" (37 cm)

*Sew using ¼" (0.7 cm) seam allowance,
unless otherwise noted.*

CUTTING INSTRUCTIONS

Trace and cut out the templates on page 122 (refer to page 6 for instructions on using templates). Cut the following fabric pieces adding ¼" (0.7 cm) seam allowance:

- 12 petal A pieces of assorted scraps (cut on the bias)
- 12 petal B pieces of assorted scraps (cut on the bias)
- 12 petal C pieces of assorted scraps (cut on the bias)
- 12 leaf pieces of assorted scraps (cut on the bias)
- 1 bottom of fabric D
- 1 bottom lining of lining fabric

Cut out the following pieces, which do not have templates, according to the measurements below (these measurements include seam allowance):

Fabric C:
- Fabric C (cut 2): 6 ¾" x 13 ½" (16.9 x 34.4 cm)

Fabric D:
- Fabric D (cut 2): 2 ½" x 13 ½" (6.4 x 34.4 cm)

Fabric B:
- Fabric B (cut 2): 1 ⅛" x 13 ½" (2.9 x 34.4 cm)
- Bias strips: 1 yard (1 m) of 1 ½" (3.5 cm) wide strips
- Handle bias strips: 1 ¾ yards (1.75 m) of 1 ½" (3.5 cm) wide strips

Fabric A:
- Fabric A (cut 2): 2 ¼" x 13 ½" (5.9 x 34.4 cm)
- Handles (cut 4): 2" x 15" (4.8 x 38.4 cm)

Lining fabric:
- Lining (cut 2): 11 ½" x 14 ½" (29.2 x 37 cm)
- Tabs (cut 4): 2" x 3 ¼" (5.4 x 8.4 cm)

CONSTRUCTION STEPS

1. Align two petal A pieces with right sides together. Layer on top of a piece of batting cut out in the shape of petal A. Sew, leaving an opening. Trim the excess seam allowance and turn right side out through the opening. Ladder stitch the opening closed. Running stitch to gather the bottom of the petal, stitching as close to the edge as possible (refer to the template on page 121 for placement). Use this process to make 6 each of petals A, B, and C.

2. Align two leaf pieces with right sides together. Layer on top of a piece of batting cut out in the shape of the leaf. Sew, leaving an opening. Make clips in the curved sections of the seam allowance. Turn right side out through the opening. Ladder stitch the opening closed. Quilt a line down the center of the leaf (refer to template on page 121 for placement). Fold the leaf in half and hemstitch together along the bottom. Use this process to make a total of six leaves.

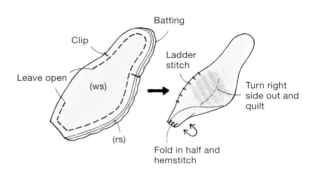

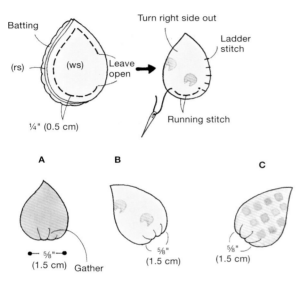

3. Mark the appliqué placement on each Fabric C piece (refer to the diagram on page 21). Cut six ½" x 4" (1.3 x 10 cm) stem pieces of assorted scraps on the bias. Fold one stem piece in half with right sides facing out. Sew along the long edge using ¼" (0.5 cm) seam allowance, leaving the bottom ¼" (0.5 cm) open. Align the stem piece with Fabric C so that the seam is not visible. Hemstitch the long edge of the stem to Fabric C. Fold the bottom of the stem under and hemstitch to Fabric C. Insert three strands of yarn into the stem. Use this same process to make and attach a total of six stems.

4. Sew pieces A, B, and D to piece C to assemble the bag top. Layer the top, batting, and lining. Quilt as shown in the diagram on page 21. Trim both sides so the piece tapers in ½" (1.3 cm) from top to bottom. This will be the front. Follow the same process to assemble the back, but leave the lining with ½" (1.2 cm) extra seam allowance along the sides and bottom.

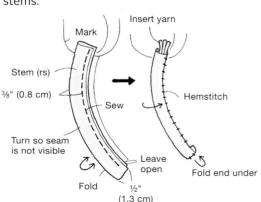

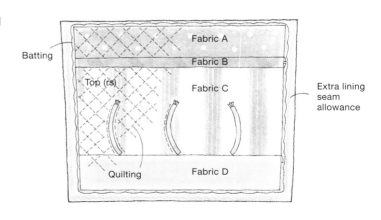

5. Use the technique shown on page 16 to sew the front and back together along the sides and finish the seam allowances using the lining.

6. Layer the bottom, batting, and lining. Quilt with ¾" (2 cm) squares. Use the technique shown on page 16 to sew the bottom to the bag and finish the seam allowance using the lining.

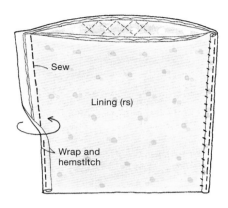

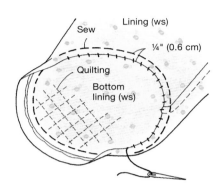

Refer to page 11 for instructions on finishing the seam allowances using lining.

7. Appliqué the petals and leaves to the bag to complete the six flowers (refer to the templates on page 122 for placement).

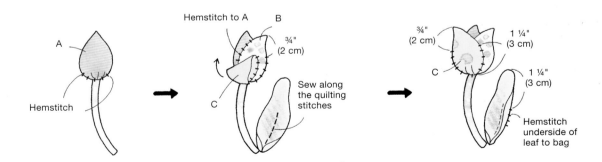

8. Use the bias strips to bind the bag opening. Embroider the Fabric B strip as shown in the diagram on page 21.

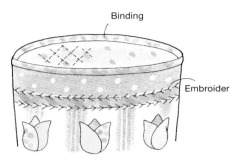

9. Layer a handle piece, batting, and another handle piece. Quilt with two horizontal lines about $\frac{3}{8}$" (1.1 cm) in from the seam allowance on each long edge. Use the handle bias strips to bind the long edges. Trim each short edge so the handle tapers in $\frac{3}{4}$" (2 cm) from top to bottom. Fold the handle in half and whipstitch the edges together for 2" (5 cm) at the center. Repeat process to make to make another handle.

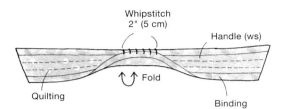

10. Sew the short end of each handle to the bag lining 1 $\frac{1}{4}$" (3 cm) below the binding (refer to the diagram on page 21 for placement). Hemstitch the tabs to the lining in order to cover the handle seam allowances.

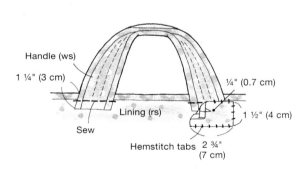

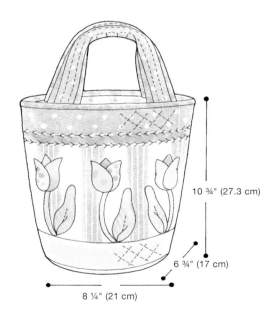

A patchwork pocket on the back of the bag is perfect for storing keys, lip gloss, and other essentials.

4 Appliquéd Tulip Purse

I have a confession to make: I have hundreds of pieces of taupe fabric in my stash! I love the chic effect created by combining neutral fabrics, but lately, I have enjoyed incorporating brighter colors into my work. Cheerful pinks, yellows, and blues are perfectly suited for this floral bag, which was inspired by tulips swaying in the wind.

For a special touch, this beautiful bag is embellished with delicate beads.

MATERIALS

- **Appliqué and patchwork fabric:** Assorted scraps
- **Main fabric:** ¼ yard of plaid fabric
- **Accent fabric:** ½ yard of dark brown fabric
- **Lining fabric:** ⅓ yard of print fabric
- **Batting:** 15 ¾" x 43 ¼" (40 x 110 cm)

- **Lightweight fusible interfacing:** 2 ¾" x 4 ¼" (7 x 11 cm)
- 31 ½" (80 cm) of ¼" (0.6 cm) wide dark brown trim
- 50 small glass beads
- One 8" (20 cm) zipper

- 19 ¾" (50 cm) of ¼" (0.5 cm) diameter string
- One cord stopper
- One set of 20" (50 cm) handles
- No. 25 embroidery floss in dark brown

PATCHWORK DIAGRAM

FRONT

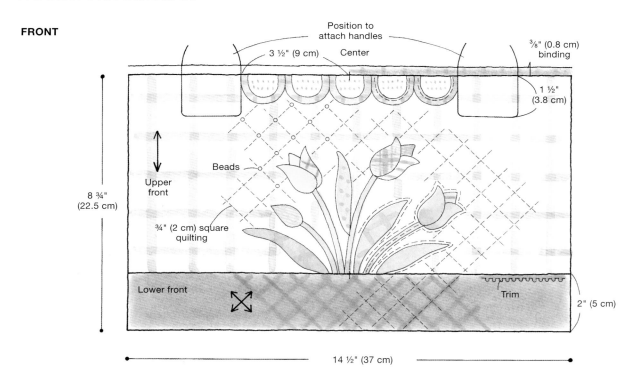

Position to attach handles

3 ½" (9 cm) Center

⅜" (0.8 cm) binding

1 ½" (3.8 cm)

Beads

Upper front

8 ¾" (22.5 cm)

¾" (2 cm) square quilting

Lower front

Trim

2" (5 cm)

14 ½" (37 cm)

BACK

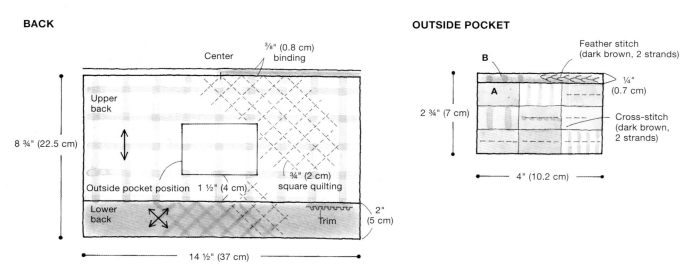

Center

⅜" (0.8 cm) binding

Upper back

8 ¾" (22.5 cm)

Outside pocket position   1 ½" (4 cm)

¾" (2 cm) square quilting

Lower back

Trim

2" (5 cm)

14 ½" (37 cm)

OUTSIDE POCKET

Feather stitch (dark brown, 2 strands)

B

A

¼" (0.7 cm)

2 ¾" (7 cm)

Cross-stitch (dark brown, 2 strands)

4" (10.2 cm)

BOTTOM

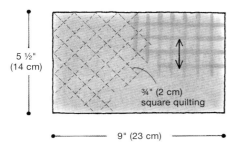

5 ½" (14 cm)

¾" (2 cm) square quilting

9" (23 cm)

Sew using ¼" (0.7 cm) seam allowance, unless otherwise noted.

CUTTING INSTRUCTIONS

Trace and cut out the templates on page 123 (refer to page 6 for instructions on using templates). Cut the following fabric pieces adding ¼" (0.7 cm) seam allowance:

- 9 **A** pieces of assorted scraps
- 1 **B** piece of accent fabric
- Appliqué tulip pieces of assorted scraps
- 5 outer scallops of accent fabric
- 5 inner scallops of assorted scraps

Cut out the following pieces, which do not have templates, according to the measurements below (these measurements include seam allowance):

Lightweight fusible interfacing:
- Pocket interfacing: 2 ¾" x 4" (7 x 10.2 cm)

Lining fabric:
- Pocket lining: 3 ¼" x 4 ½" (8.4 x 11.6 cm)

- Linings (cut 2): 9 ¾" x 16" (25.2 x 41 cm)
- Bottom lining: 6" x 9 ½" (15.4 x 24.4 cm)
- Inside pocket: 6 ½" x 8 ¾" (16.4 x 22.4 cm)
- Tabs (cut 2): 1 ⅛" x 1 ¼" (2.9 x 3.4 cm)

Main fabric:
- Upper front/back (cut 1 of each): 7 ¼" x 15" (18.9 x 38.4 cm)

Accent fabric:
- Lower front/back (cut 1 of each): 2 ½" x 15" (6.4 x 38.4 cm)
- Bottom: 6" x 9 ½" (15.4 x 24.4 cm)
- Bias strips: 1 yard (1 m) of 1 ½" (3.5 cm) wide bias strips

CONSTRUCTION STEPS

1. To make the outside pocket, sew A pieces into columns of three, then sew the three columns together. Press the seam allowances in the directions indicated by the arrows. Sew piece B to the top. Adhere the pocket interfacing to the wrong side. Sew the pocket and lining with right sides together, leaving an opening. Turn the pocket right side out and hemstitch the opening closed. Quilt, then embroider the pocket as shown in the diagram on page 26.

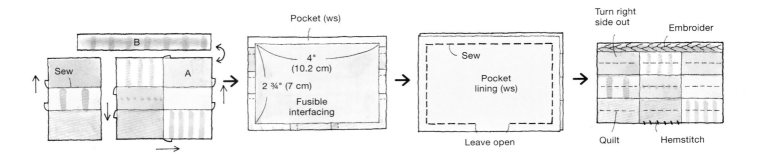

2. Appliqué the tulip pieces to the bag front and embroider the stems as indicated on the templates. Appliqué the outer and inner scallops to the bag front using a hemstitch (refer to the diagram on page 26 for placement). Sew the upper and lower pieces together to make the bag front and back.

3. Layer the front, batting, and lining. Stitch in the ditch around the tulip appliqué, then quilt as shown in the diagram on page 26. Follow the same process to quilt the back. Use the technique shown on page 16 to sew the front and back together along the sides and finish the seam allowances using the lining.

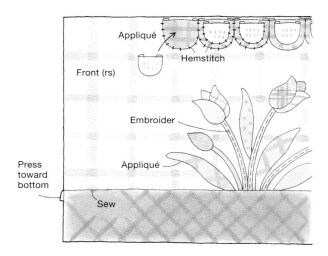

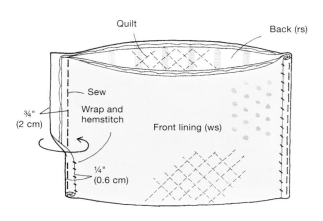

Refer to page 11 for instructions on finishing the seam allowances using lining.

4. Layer the bottom, batting, and lining. Quilt as shown in the diagram on page 26. Use the technique shown on page 16 to sew the bottom to the bag and finish the seam allowances using the lining.

5. Fold inside pocket in half with right sides together and sew around three sides, leaving an opening. Turn the pocket right side out and hemstitch the opening closed.

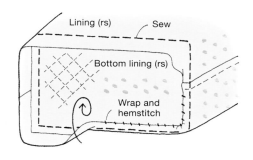

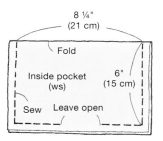

Refer to page 11 for instructions on finishing the seam allowances using lining.

6. Sew one side of the zipper to the folded edge of the pocket. Hemstitch the pocket to the inside of the bag. Fold the seam allowance under on the other side of the zipper and backstitch to the inside of the bag.

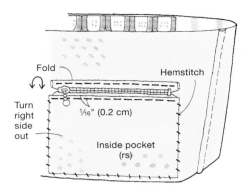

Fold

Hemstitch

Turn right side out

¹⁄₁₆" (0.2 cm)

Inside pocket (rs)

7. Use the bias strips to bind the bag opening. Thread the cord stopper onto the string so it is positioned near the center. Tie a knot to secure in place. Fold each end of the string over ¼" (0.5 cm) and hemstitch to the inside of the bag, just below the binding. Hemstitch the tabs to the lining.

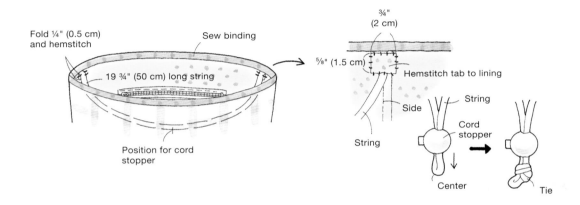

Fold ¼" (0.5 cm) and hemstitch

Sew binding

19 ¾" (50 cm) long string

Position for cord stopper

¾" (2 cm)

⁵⁄₈" (1.5 cm)

Hemstitch tab to lining

Side

String

String

Cord stopper

Center

Tie

8. Hemstitch the outside pocket to the bag back (refer to the diagram on page 26 for placement). Backstitch the trim to the bag, covering the seam between the upper and lower sections. Sew the beads to the front of the bag as shown in the diagram below. Backstitch the handles to the bag using two strands of quilting thread (refer to the diagram on page 26 for placement).

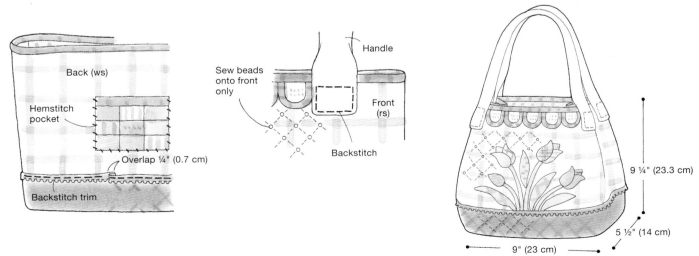

Back (ws)

Hemstitch pocket

Overlap ¼" (0.7 cm)

Backstitch trim

Sew beads onto front only

Handle

Front (rs)

Backstitch

9 ¼" (23.3 cm)

5 ½" (14 cm)

9" (23 cm)

Two-Way Hexagon Purse

⑤

My favorite bag designs are often the ones that are the most versatile. I love that this bag can be carried by the handles or worn over the shoulder. With its hidden pocket and dual handles, this bag is perfect for travel.

The English paper pieced hexies form a secret zippered pocket.

MATERIALS

- **Patchwork fabric:** Assorted scraps
- **Main fabric:** ½ yard of striped fabric
- **Lining fabric:** ¾ yard of print fabric
- **Batting:** 11 ¾" x 23 ¾" (30 x 60 cm)

- One 10" (25.5 cm) zipper
- One 11" (28 cm) zipper
- Two ⅝" (1.6 cm) diameter cover buttons

- Two ⅜" (1 cm) diameter D-rings
- One set of 13" (33 cm) handles
- One 44"-51" (110-130 cm) adjustable shoulder strap with metal swivel hooks

PATCHWORK DIAGRAM

Close Up View

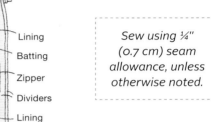

Sew using ¼" (0.7 cm) seam allowance, unless otherwise noted.

FRONT

11" (28 cm) zipper opening

Position to attach handles

2 ¼" (5.5 cm)

⅜" (0.8 cm) binding

Center

Upper front (rs)

⅜" (1 cm) quilting

10" (25.5 cm) zipper opening

⅜" (0.8 cm) binding

2 ½" (6 cm)

¼" (0.7 cm)

¼" (0.7 cm)

¼" (0.5 cm) quilting

9 ¾" (24.7 cm)

Pocket (rs)

A

7" (17.9 cm)

10" (25.5 cm)

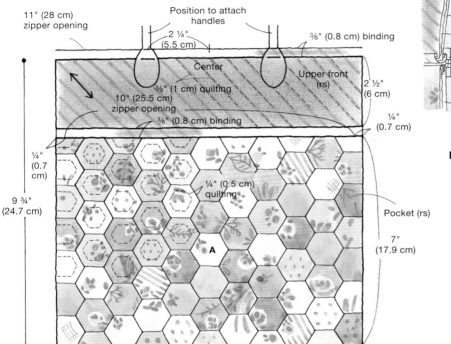

BACK/BOTTOM

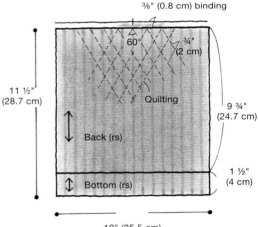

⅜" (0.8 cm) binding

60°

¾" (2 cm)

Quilting

11 ½" (28.7 cm)

Back (rs)

9 ¾" (24.7 cm)

1 ½" (4 cm)

Bottom (rs)

10" (25.5 cm)

CUTTING INSTRUCTIONS

Trace and cut out the template on page 121 (refer to page 6 for instructions on using templates). Cut the following fabric pieces adding ¼" (0.7 cm) seam allowance:

- 77 **A** pieces of assorted scraps

Cut out the following pieces, which do not have templates, according to the measurements below (these measurements include seam allowance):

Lining fabric:
- Pocket lining: 7 ½" x 10 ½" (19.3 x 26.9 cm)
- Upper front lining: 3" x 10 ½" (7.4 x 26.9 cm)
- Dividers (cut 2): 10 ¼" x 10 ½" (26.1 x 26.9 cm)
- Back lining: 11 ½" x 12 ½" (29.5 x 31.4 cm)

Main fabric:
- Upper front: 3" x 10 ½" (7.4 x 26.9 cm)
- Bias strips: 1 yard (1 m) of 1 ½" (3.5 cm) wide bias strips
- Back: 10 ¼" x 10 ½" (26.1 x 26.9 cm)
- Bottom: 2" x 10 ½" (5.4 x 26.9 cm)
- Tabs: 1 ½" x 1 ½" (4 x 4 cm)

Assorted scraps:
- Covered buttons (cut 2): 1 ¼" (3 cm) diameter circles
- Zipper charm: 1 ½" (4 cm) diameter circle

CONSTRUCTION STEPS

1. Make the pocket top using the English paper piecing technique shown in the diagram on page 89. Trim the pocket top into a 7 ½" x 10 ½" (19.3 x 26.9 cm) rectangle. Align the pocket top and lining with right sides together. Layer a piece of batting underneath. Sew along the top edge, then turn right side out. Quilt each hexagon as shown in the diagram on page 31.

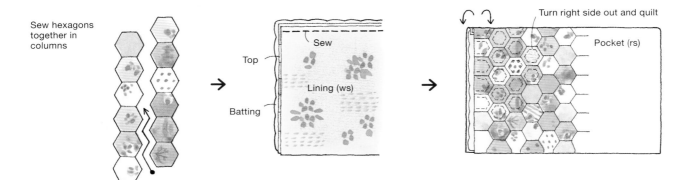

2. Layer the upper front, batting, and lining. Quilt with diagonal lines spaced ⅜" (1 cm) apart. Use the bias strips to bind the bottom edge of the quilted upper front.

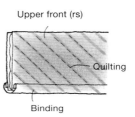

3. Refer to step 3 on page 40 to attach the 10" (25.5 cm) zipper to the upper front and pocket. (**Note:** You may need to trim excess zipper length.)

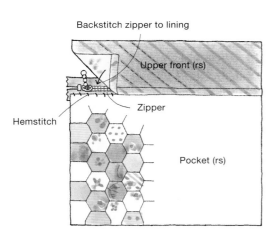

4. Align the two dividers with right sides facing out. Layer the bag front from step 3 on top of the dividers. Baste together around all four sides. Hemstitch the binding to the pocket for ¼" (0.7 cm) at each end of the zipper opening, as represented by the ☆.

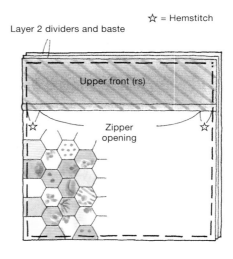

5. With right sides together, sew the bottom to the back. Layer this piece on top of the batting and lining. Quilt as shown in the diagram on page 31. Align the bag front and bottom with right sides together. (**Note:** The lining will be larger.) Sew together along the bag bottom.

6. Use the technique shown on page 11 to finish the bottom seam allowance using the lining. Pin the bag front and back together along the top of the bag. Use the technique shown on page 16 to sew the front and back together along the sides and finish the seam allowances using the lining.

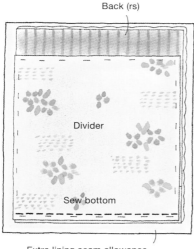

Back (rs)

Divider

Sew bottom

Extra lining seam allowance

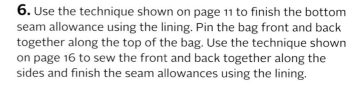

Align at top

Wrap and hemstitch

Sew

Lining (rs)

¼" (0.6 cm)

Wrap and hemstitch

¼" (0.6 cm)

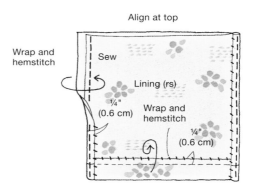

Lining (rs)

Sew

Fold and hemstitch

7. Mark each side seam 1 ½" (4 cm) above the bottom fold of the bag. Fold to align the marks with the bottom fold. Miter each corner. Fold the corner seam allowances toward the bottom and hemstitch to the lining.

8. For each tab, fold and press ⅜" (1 cm) to the wrong side on the left and right edges. With right sides facing out, fold the tabs in half. Thread a D-ring onto each tab, then fold as shown in the diagram below so the tabs measure ⅝" (1.5 cm) tall. Next, use the bias strips to bind the bag opening. Sew the 11" (28 cm) zipper to the binding as shown below. (**Note:** You may need to trim excess zipper length.) Make the covered buttons (refer to page 12) and attach to one end of the zipper. Hemstitch the tabs to the back, about ¼" (0.5 cm) in from the side seams. Backstitch the handles to the bag using two strands of quilting thread (refer to the diagram on page 31 for placement). Make the zipper charm (refer to page 12).

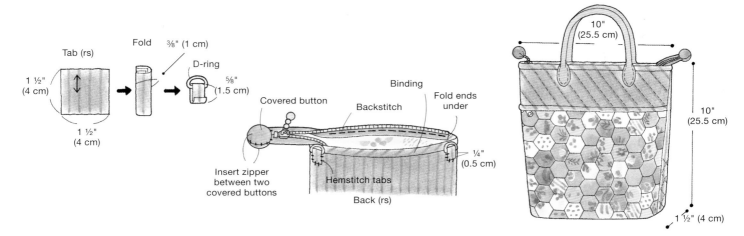

Tab (rs)

Fold

⅜" (1 cm)

D-ring

⅝" (1.5 cm)

1 ½" (4 cm)

1 ½" (4 cm)

Covered button

Binding

Backstitch

Fold ends under

Insert zipper between two covered buttons

Hemstitch tabs

¼" (0.5 cm)

Back (rs)

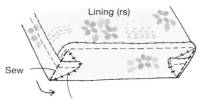

10" (25.5 cm)

10" (25.5 cm)

1 ½" (4 cm)

6 Cross-Body Bouquet Bag

This humble purse has accompanied
me to workshops and events all
around the world. It is the perfect
size for carrying essential travel
items, such as my passport,
smartphone, and glasses. I love
the way I can wear it across my
body and it looks great with all
my favorite dresses.

MATERIALS

- **Appliqué fabric:** Assorted scraps
- **Main fabric:** ½ yard of light green fabric
- **Accent fabric:** ¼ yard of beige fabric
- **Bottom fabric:** ⅛ yard of brown fabric
- **Lining fabric:** ½ yard of print fabric

- **Batting:** 11 ¾" x 13 ¾" (30 x 35 cm)
- One 8" (20.5 cm) zipper
- One 11" (28 cm) zipper
- Two ¾" (1.8 cm) diameter cover buttons
- Two ½" (1.2 cm) diameter D-rings

- One 47" (120 cm) shoulder strap with metal swivel hooks
- No. 25 embroidery floss in green
- Candlewicking floss in white

PATCHWORK DIAGRAM

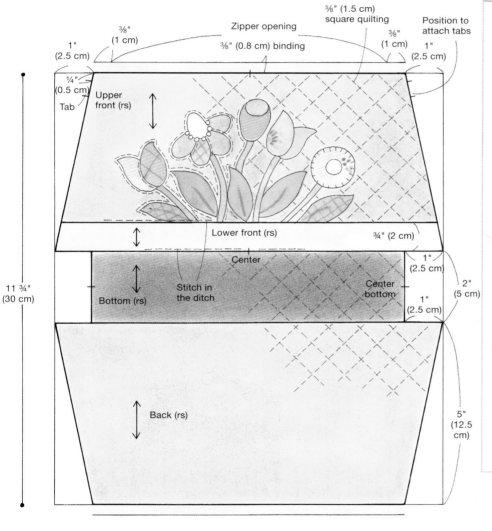

Trace and cut out the templates on page 121 (refer to page 6 for instructions on using templates). Cut the following fabric pieces adding ¼" (0.7 cm) seam allowance:

- Appliqué flower pieces of assorted scraps

Cut out the following pieces, which do not have templates, according to the measurements below (these measurements include seam allowance):

Main fabric:
- Upper front: 4 ¾" x 10 ¾" (11.9 x 27.4 cm)
- Back: 5 ½" x 10 ¾" (13.9 x 27.4 cm)
- Tabs (cut 2): 1 ¼" x 2" (3 x 4.8 cm)

Accent fabric:
- Lower front: 1 ¼" x 10 ¾" (3.4 x 27.4 cm)
- Binding strips (cut lengthwise): ¾ yard (0.75 m) of 1 ½" (3.5 cm) wide strips
- Back: 10 ¼" x 10 ½" (26.1 x 26.9 cm)

Bottom fabric:
- Bottom: 2 ½" x 10 ¾" (6.4 x 27.4 cm)

Assorted scraps:
- Covered buttons (cut 2): 1 ½" (3.5 cm) diameter circles
- Zipper charm: 1 ½" (4 cm) diameter circle

Sew using ¼" (0.7 cm) seam allowance, unless otherwise noted.

CONSTRUCTION STEPS

1. Appliqué the flowers to the upper front and embroider as indicated on the templates. Attach the lower front, bottom, and back following the placement indicated in the diagram on page 35. Trim the front and back so they taper in 1" (2.5 cm) from bottom to top. Cut the lining in the shape of the completed top, adding ½" (1.2 cm) extra seam allowance along each side. (**Note:** You don't need to add extra seam allowance to the top or bottom.) Layer the top, batting, and lining. Stitch in the ditch and quilt with ⅝" (1.5 cm) squares.

2. For each tab, fold and press ½" (1.2 cm) to the wrong side on the left and right edges. With right sides facing out, fold each tab in half. Topstitch along each long edge, stitching as close to the fold as possible. Thread the D-rings onto the tabs. Fold the tabs in half and baste the edges together.

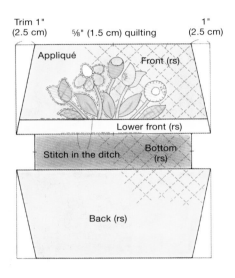

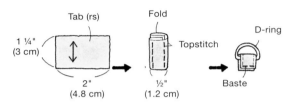

3. Pin the tabs to the right side of the bag front, about ½" (1.2 cm) from the top. Fold the bag in half with right sides together. Use the technique shown on page 16 to sew the front and back together along the sides and finish the seam allowances using the lining. Align each side seam with the bottom fold. Miter each corner by sewing a 2" (5 cm) long seam.

4. Use the binding strips to bind the bag opening. Sew the zipper to the binding as shown below. Make the covered buttons and attach to one end of the zipper (refer to page 12). Make the zipper charm (refer to page 12).

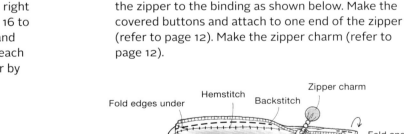

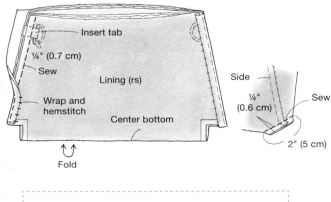

Refer to page 11 for instructions on finishing the seam allowances using lining.

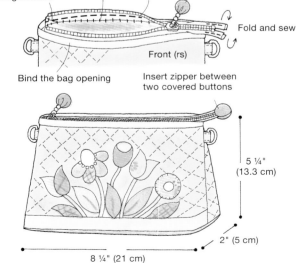

⑦ Newsprint Backpack

Every year, I receive requests for a backpack pattern, so this design is dedicated to my loyal and patient customers. With its durable straps, inner divider, and zipper openings, this bag is perfect for travel.

1

2

1. Dual zippers allow the bag to open from both directions. I also used a zipper for the front pocket for added security.

2. This design uses a premade strap, which is easy to install and creates a professional-looking finish.

MATERIALS

- **Patchwork fabric:**
  - A: 32 assorted scraps
  - B & C: ¼ yard of text print
- **Main fabric:** ½ yard of taupe stripe
- **Accent fabric:** ⅔ yard of taupe plaid
- **Lining fabric:** ¾ yard of print fabric

- **Batting:** 19 ¾" x 39 ½" (50 x 100 cm)
- **Lightweight fusible interfacing:** 11 ¾" x 13 ¾" (30 x 35 cm)
- Two 8" (20 cm) zippers (for bag opening)
- One 10" (25 cm) zipper (for pocket)
- Four 1 ¼" (3 cm) diameter cover buttons

- One ¾" (2 cm) diameter magnetic snap set
- One 22"-39" (55-98 cm) adjustable backpack shoulder strap set
- No. 25 embroidery floss in dark brown

PATCHWORK DIAGRAM

FRONT

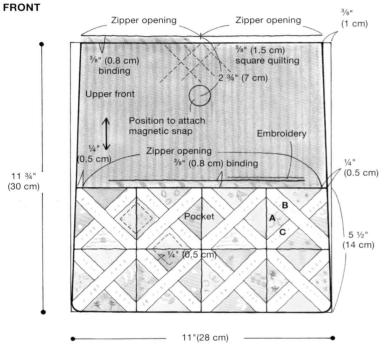

GUSSET

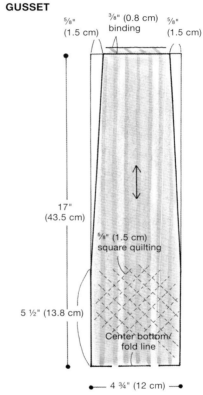

BACK

FLAP

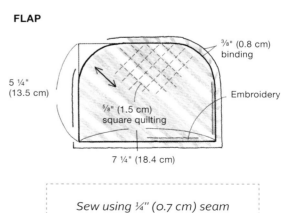

Sew using ¼" (0.7 cm) seam allowance, unless otherwise noted.

CUTTING INSTRUCTIONS

Trace and cut out the templates on page 123 (refer to page 6 for instructions on using templates). Cut the following fabric pieces adding ¼" (0.7 cm) seam allowance:

- 32 **A** pieces of assorted scraps
- 8 **B** pieces of text print
- 16 **C** pieces of text print

Cut out the following pieces, which do not have templates, according to the measurements below (these measurements include seam allowance):

Lining fabric:
- Pocket lining: 6" x 11 ½" (15.4 x 29.4 cm)
- Upper front lining: 6 ¾" x 11 ½" (17.4 x 29.4 cm)
- Divider pieces (cut 2): 11 ½" x 12 ¼" (29.4 x 31.4 cm)
- Back lining: 11 ½" x 12 ¼" (29.4 x 31.4 cm)
- Gusset lining (cut on the fold): 6 ¼" x 17 ½" (16 x 44.9 cm)

- Flap lining: 5 ¾" x 7 ¾" (14.9 x 19.8 cm)

Main fabric
- Upper front: 6 ¾" x 11 ½" (17.4 x 29.4 cm)
- Back: 11 ½" x 12 ¼" (29.4 x 31.4 cm)

Accent fabric
- Bias strips: 1 ¾ yards (1.75 m) of 1 ½" (3.5 cm) wide bias strips
- Gusset (cut on the fold): 5 ¼" x 17 ½" (13.4 x 44.9 cm)
- Flap: 5 ¾" x 7 ¾" (14.9 x 19.8 cm)

Assorted scraps
- Covered buttons (cut 4): 1 ¾" (4.5 cm) diameter circles

CONSTRUCTION STEPS

1. Sew two A pieces to each C piece. Sew a B piece to one of the sets, then attach another set. Repeat process to make eight blocks. Sew the blocks together in two rows of four to create the pocket top.

2. Align the pocket top and lining with right sides together. Layer a piece of batting underneath. Sew along one long edge. Trim the batting seam allowance and turn right side out. Quilt using ¼" (0.5 cm) seam allowance as shown in the diagram below.

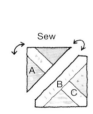

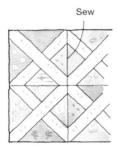

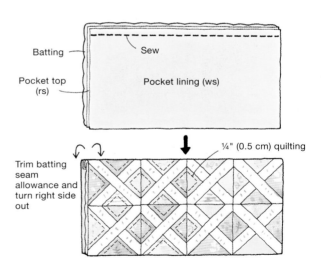

3. Layer the upper front, batting, and lining. Quilt with ⅝" (1.5 cm) squares. Align the quilted upper front and pocket. Trim both sides, so the piece tapers in ⅜" (1 cm) from bottom to top. Use the bias strips to bind the lower edge of the quilted upper front. Embroider the binding as shown in the diagram at right. Sew one side of the zipper to the pocket and the other side to the quilted upper front.

Refer to page 12 for instructions on installing a zipper.

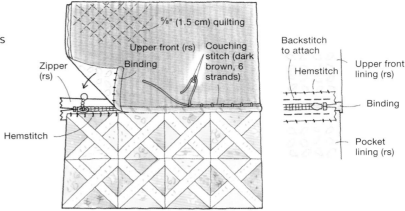

4. Adhere fusible interfacing to the wrong side of one divider piece. With right sides facing out, layer another divider piece underneath. Quilt with 2" (5 cm) squares. Using the bag front as a template, trim the divider to match. Align the bag front on top of the divider and baste around all four sides. Hemstitch the binding to the pocket for ¼" (0.5 cm) at each end of the zipper opening.

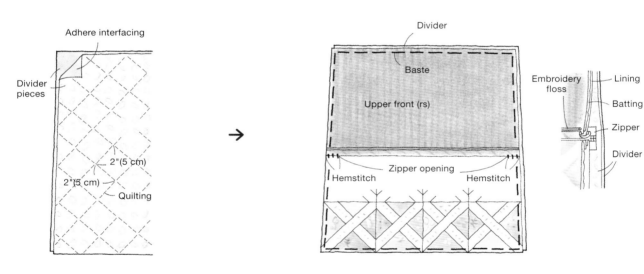

5. Layer the back, batting, and lining. Quilt with ⅝" (1.5 cm) squares. Follow the same process to quilt the gusset. Trim both sides of the back, so the piece tapers in ⅜" (1 cm) from bottom to top. Fold the gusset in half and trim both sides so the piece tapers in ⅝" (1.5 cm), starting 5 ½" (13.8 cm) from the fold. Use the technique shown on page 11 to sew the gusset to the bag front and back and finish the seam allowances using the lining.

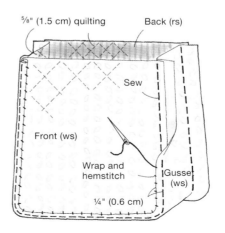

6. Use the bias strips to bind the bag opening. Sew the two zippers to the binding as shown below. Make the covered buttons (refer to page 12) and attach to the zipper ends. Sew the male magnetic snap to the upper front (refer to the diagram on page 38 for placement).

7. Layer the flap, batting, and lining. Quilt with ⅝" (1.5 cm) squares. Trim the corners of the flap into a rounded shape. Use the bias strips to bind the flap (refer to page 10 for mitered corner instructions). Embroider the binding as shown in the diagram below.

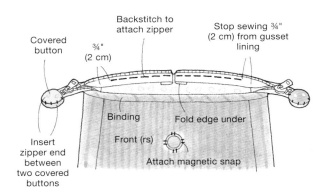

Covered button

¾" (2 cm)

Backstitch to attach zipper

Stop sewing ¾" (2 cm) from gusset lining

Binding

Fold edge under

Front (rs)

Attach magnetic snap

Insert zipper end between two covered buttons

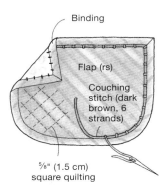

Binding

Flap (rs)

Couching stitch (dark brown, 6 strands)

⅝" (1.5 cm) square quilting

8. Hemstitch the flap to the back (refer to the diagram on page 38 for placement). Sew the female magnetic snap to the flap. Running stitch for 6" (15 cm) from the top, stitching through both the back and gusset. Use ¼" (0.5 cm) seam allowance. Backstitch the shoulder strap set to the back using two strands of quilting thread (refer to the diagram on page 38 for placement).

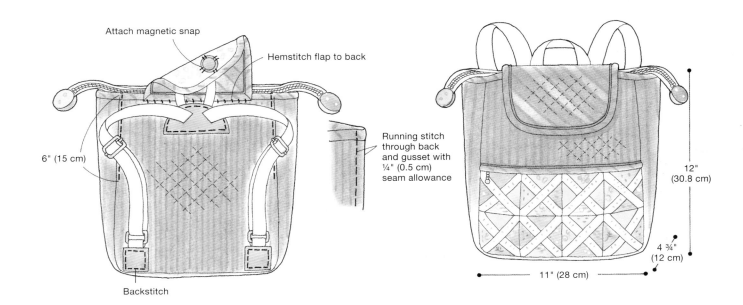

Attach magnetic snap

Hemstitch flap to back

6" (15 cm)

Backstitch

Running stitch through back and gusset with ¼" (0.5 cm) seam allowance

12" (30.8 cm)

4 ¾" (12 cm)

11" (28 cm)

⑧ Swivel Hook Tote

A simple metal buckle serves as the focal point of this design. When you have a lot to carry, simply unhook the buckle to use the bag as a conventional tote. With two silhouette options, this bag is both versatile and stylish. Customize your tote by embroidering your own initial.

FRONT

BACK

When you unhook the buckle, this bag transforms into a traditional tote bag.

MATERIALS

- **Patchwork fabric:** Assorted scraps
- **Text fabric:** ¼ yard of text print fabric
- **Main fabric:** ¾ yard of solid beige fabric
- **Lining fabric:** ⅝ yard of print fabric

- **Batting:** 21 ¾" x 39 ½" (55 x 100 cm)
- One metal swivel hook with D-ring and 1" x 2" (2.5 x 5 cm) leather tab

- One metal D-ring with 1" x 1 ¼" (2.5 x 3 cm) leather tab
- One set of 25" (63 cm) handles
- Candlewicking floss in white

PATCHWORK DIAGRAM

FRONT

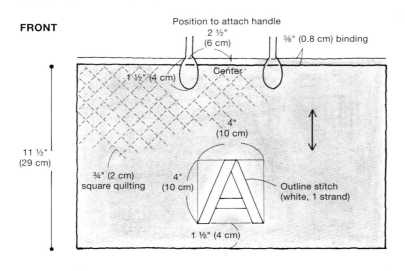

BACK

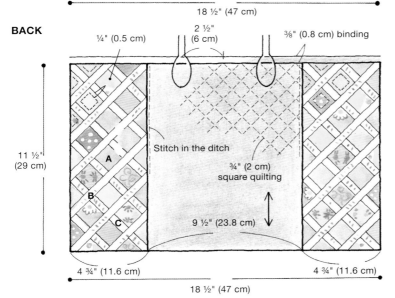

BOTTOM

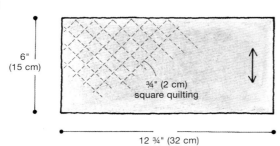

CUTTING INSTRUCTIONS

Trace and cut out the templates on page 124 (refer to page 6 for instructions on using templates). Cut the following fabric pieces adding ¼" (0.7 cm) seam allowance:

- 54 **A** pieces of assorted scraps
- 12 **B** pieces of text print
- 40 **C** pieces of text print
- Letter template of main fabric

Cut out the following pieces, which do not have templates, according to the measurements below (these measurements include seam allowance):

Main fabric:
- Center back: 10" x 12" (25.2 x 30.4 cm)
- Front: 12" x 19" (30.4 x 48.4 cm)
- Bottom: 6 ½" x 13 ¼" (16.4 x 33.4 cm)
- Bias strips: 1 ¼ yards (1.25 m) of 1 ½" (3.5 cm) wide bias strips

Lining fabric:
- Back lining: 12 ½" x 20" (31.7 x 51 cm)
- Front lining 12 ½" x 19" (31.7 x 48.4 cm)
- Bottom lining: 6 ½" x 13 ¼" (16.4 x 33.4 cm)
- Bias strips: ½ yard (0.5 m) of 1 ½" (3.5 cm) wide bias strips

Sew using ¼" (0.7 cm) seam allowance, unless otherwise noted.

CONSTRUCTION STEPS

1. Sew pieces A-C together to create the two patchwork panels. Trim each patchwork panel into a 5 ¼" x 12" (13 x 30.4 cm) rectangle. Sew a patchwork panel to each side of the center back piece. Layer the back, batting, and lining. Quilt as shown in the diagram below.

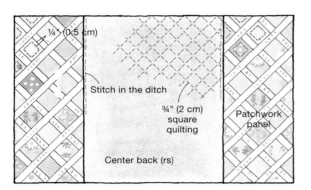

¼" (0.5 cm)

Stitch in the ditch

¾" (2 cm) square quilting

Patchwork panel

Center back (rs)

2. Use the template to appliqué and embroider the letter to the front (refer to the diagram on page 43 for placement). Layer the front, batting, and lining. Quilt with ¾" (2 cm) squares.

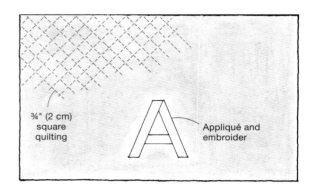

¾" (2 cm) square quilting

Appliqué and embroider

3. Use the technique shown on page 16 to sew the front and back together along the sides and finish the seam allowances using the lining. Layer the bottom, batting, and lining. Quilt as shown in the diagram on page 43. Use the technique shown on page 16 to sew the bottom to the bag and finish the seam allowances using the lining. Use the lining bias strips to bind the bottom side seam allowances.

Refer to page 11 for instructions on finishing the seam allowances using lining.

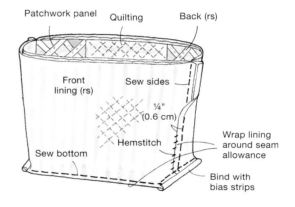

Patchwork panel   Quilting   Back (rs)

Front lining (rs)   Sew sides

¼" (0.6 cm)

Hemstitch

Sew bottom

Wrap lining around seam allowance

Bind with bias strips

4. Use the main fabric bias strips to bind the bag opening. Align the metal swivel hook with leather tab on the diagonal at the upper left corner of the bag back. Backstitch the leather tab to the bag. Backstitch the metal D-ring with leather tab to the upper right corner of the bag back. Backstitch the handles to the bag using two strands of quilting thread (refer to the diagrams on page 43 for placement).

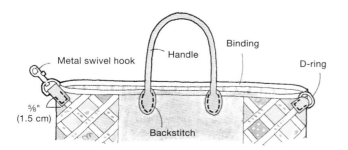

Metal swivel hook   Handle   Binding   D-ring

⅝" (1.5 cm)

Backstitch

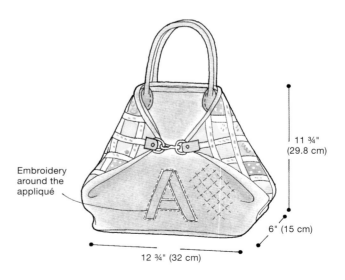

Embroidery around the appliqué

11 ¾" (29.8 cm)

6" (15 cm)

12 ¾" (32 cm)

9 Classic Bowling Bag

The design for this bag was inspired by the light brown striped fabric. It may seem like a run-of-the-mill striped fabric at first glance, but if you look closely, you'll notice various colors of thread woven together to create this beautiful textile. This unique shell-shaped bag maximizes the use of this humble brown fabric.

MATERIALS

- **Patchwork fabric:** Assorted scraps
- **Main fabric:** ¾ yard of light brown striped fabric
- **Accent fabric:** ¼ yard of dark brown fabric
- **Lining fabric:** ⅝ yard of print fabric
- **Batting:** 19 ¾" x 27 ½" (50 x 70 cm)
- Two 10" (25.5 cm) zippers
- One set of 22" (55 cm) handles
- No. 25 embroidery floss in dark brown

PATCHWORK DIAGRAM

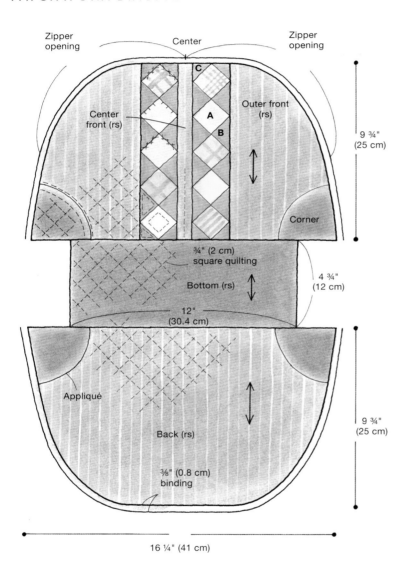

Zipper opening
Center
Zipper opening

Center front (rs)

Outer front (rs)

C
A
B

Corner

9 ¾" (25 cm)

¾" (2 cm) square quilting

Bottom (rs)

4 ¾" (12 cm)

12" (30.4 cm)

Appliqué

Back (rs)

⅜" (0.8 cm) binding

9 ¾" (25 cm)

16 ¼" (41 cm)

Sew using ¼" (0.7 cm) seam allowance, unless otherwise noted.

CUTTING INSTRUCTIONS

Trace and cut out the templates on Pattern Sheet B (refer to page 6 for instructions on using templates). Cut the following fabric pieces adding ¼" (0.7 cm) seam allowance:

- 10 **A** pieces of assorted scraps
- 16 **B** pieces of accent fabric
- 8 **C** pieces of accent fabric
- 1 center front of main fabric
- 2 outer fronts of main fabric
- 4 corners of accent fabric
- 1 back of main fabric

Cut out the following pieces, which do not have templates, according to the measurements below (these measurements include seam allowance):

Accent fabric:
- Bottom: 5 ¼" x 12 ½" (13.4 x 31.8 cm)

Main fabric:
- Bias strips: 2 yards (2 m) of 1 ½" (3.5 cm) wide bias strips

Assorted scraps:
- Zipper charms (cut 2): 1 ½" (4 cm) diameter circles

CONSTRUCTION STEPS

1. Sew pieces A-C together to create the two patchwork panels. Sew a patchwork panel to each side of the center front piece. Sew an outer front to the remaining side of each patchwork piece. Appliqué the corners to the front and back (refer to the template for placement).

2. Sew the front, bottom, and back together following the placement indicated in the diagram on page 46. Cut the lining in the shape of the completed bag top. Layer the top, batting, and lining. Quilt as shown in the diagram on page 46. Embroider the patchwork panels and corners as indicated on the templates.

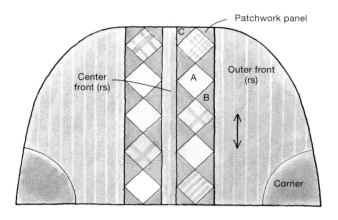

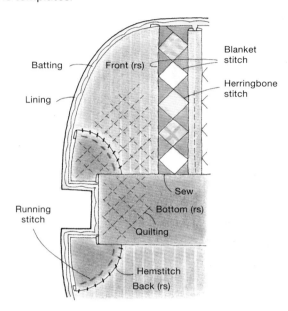

3. Use the bias strips to bind the curved edge of both the front and back. Sew the two zippers to the binding as shown below. Fold the bag in half with right sides facing out. Use ladder stitch to sew the sides of the bag together beneath the zipper (refer to page 11). Turn the bag inside out. Align each side seam with the bottom fold. Miter each corner. Use the bias strips to bind the corner seam allowances. Backstitch the handles to the bag using two strands of quilting thread (refer to the template for placement). Make the zipper charms (refer to page 12).

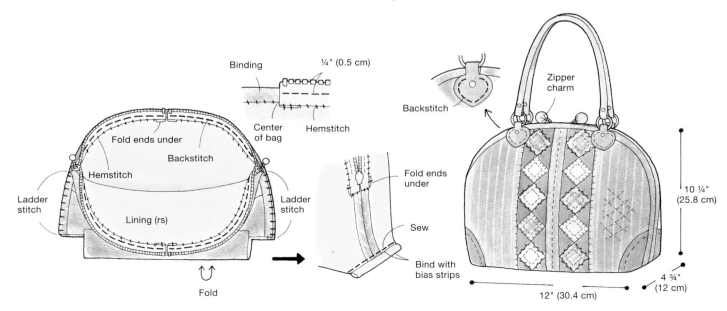

I particularly love the combination of colors and patterns in this bag and pouch set. The green floral pattern interacts with the gradated green and soft pink plaid fabrics and creates a harmonious effect. I can't wait to use this combination of fabrics for future projects.

The pouch design matches the pocket on the tote.

The pouch bottom is shaped like a long ellipse, which makes it compact, but allows it to store a great deal.

Just sew the zipper to the bag in order to attach the pocket. This shortcut technique allows you to make pockets quickly and easily.

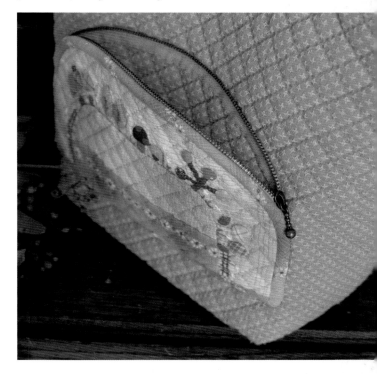

Home Sweet Home Tote

MATERIALS

- **Appliqué fabric:** Assorted scraps
- **Main fabric:** ½ yard of light green print fabric
- **Grass fabric #1:** ⅛ yard of light green plaid fabric

- **Grass fabric #2:** ⅓ yard of green floral print fabric
- **Pocket fabric:** ¼ yard of pink plaid fabric
- **Lining fabric:** ½ yard of print fabric
- **Batting:** 15 ¾" x 33 ½" (40 x 85 cm)

- One 11" (28 cm) zipper
- One set of 20" (51 cm) handles
- No. 25 embroidery floss in white, green, and brown

CUTTING INSTRUCTIONS

Trace and cut out the templates on Pattern Sheet B (refer to page 6 for instructions on using templates). Cut the following fabric pieces adding ¼" (0.7 cm) seam allowance:

- Appliqué pieces of assorted scraps
- 1 **A** piece of grass fabric #1
- 1 **B** piece of grass fabric #2
- 1 pocket of pocket fabric
- 1 pocket lining of lining fabric

Cut out the following pieces, which do not have templates, according to the measurements below (these measurements include seam allowance):

Main fabric:
- Top: 14" x 27" (35.4 x 68.4 cm)
- Binding strips (cut lengthwise): 1 yard (1 m) of 1 ½" (3.5 cm) wide strips

Lining fabric:
- Lining: 15" x 27" (36 x 68.4 cm)

Grass fabric #2:
- Bias strips: 1 yard (1 m) of 1 ½" (3.5 cm) wide bias strips

PATCHWORK DIAGRAM

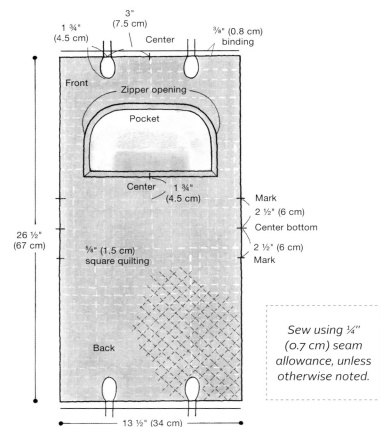

3" (7.5 cm)

1 ¾" (4.5 cm)

Center

⅜" (0.8 cm) binding

Front

Zipper opening

Pocket

Center

1 ¾" (4.5 cm)

Mark

2 ½" (6 cm)

Center bottom

2 ½" (6 cm)

Mark

26 ½" (67 cm)

⅝" (1.5 cm) square quilting

Back

13 ½" (34 cm)

Sew using ¼" (0.7 cm) seam allowance, unless otherwise noted.

CONSTRUCTION STEPS

1. Layer the top, batting, and lining. Quilt as shown in the diagram at left. Fold the bag in half with right sides together. Use the technique shown on page 16 to sew the bag together along the sides and finish the seam allowances using the lining.

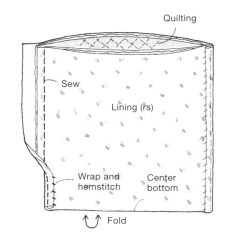

Quilting

Sew

Lining (rs)

Wrap and hemstitch

Center bottom

Fold

Refer to page 11 for instructions on finishing the seam allowances using lining.

2. Mark each side seam 2 ½" (6 cm) above and below the bottom fold of the bag. Fold to align the marks with the bottom fold. Miter each corner. Fold the corner seam allowances toward the bottom and hemstitch to the lining. Use the binding strips to bind the bag opening.

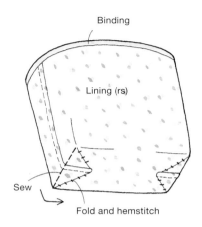

Binding

Lining (rs)

Sew

Fold and hemstitch

3. Appliqué the pieces to the pocket (refer to template for placement). Sew A and B together, then appliqué to the pocket. Layer the pocket, batting, and lining. Quilt with ⅝" (1.5 cm) squares.

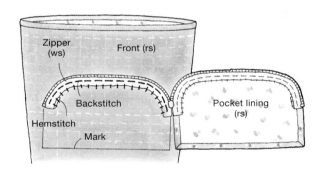

Batting

Appliqué

Sew

Lining

Quilting

4. Use the bias strips to bind the pocket (refer to page 10 for mitered corner instructions). Fold the zipper ends under and sew one side of the zipper to the binding (refer to template for placement). (**Note:** You may need to trim excess zipper length before sewing to the binding.)

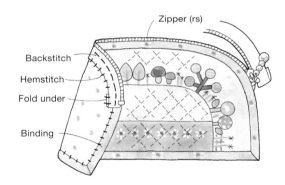

Zipper (rs)

Backstitch

Hemstitch

Fold under

Binding

5. Mark the pocket placement on the bag front following placement indicated in the diagram on page 50. Fold the zipper ends under and sew the other side of the zipper to the bag front.

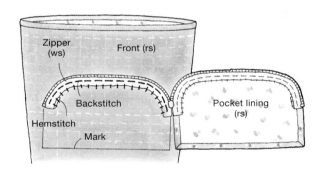

Zipper (ws)

Front (rs)

Backstitch

Hemstitch

Mark

Pocket lining (rs)

6. Hemstitch the pocket to the bag. Backstitch the handles to the bag using two strands of quilting thread (refer to the diagram on page 50 for placement).

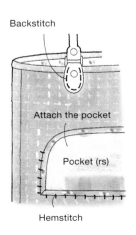

Backstitch

Attach the pocket

Pocket (rs)

Hemstitch

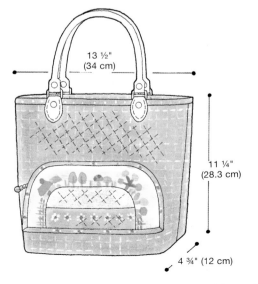

13 ½" (34 cm)

11 ¼" (28.3 cm)

4 ¾" (12 cm)

Home Sweet Home Pouch

MATERIALS

- **Appliqué fabric:** Assorted scraps
- **Main fabric:** ⅓ yard of pink plaid fabric
- **Grass fabric #1:** ⅛ yard of light green plaid fabric
- **Grass fabric #2:** ⅛ yard of green floral print fabric
- **Lining fabric:** ⅓ yard of print fabric
- **Batting:** 9 ¾" x 21 ¾" (25 x 55 cm)
- One 10" (25.5 cm) zipper
- No. 25 embroidery floss in white, green, and brown

CUTTING INSTRUCTIONS

Trace and cut out the templates on Pattern Sheet B (refer to page 6 for instructions on using templates). Cut the following fabric pieces adding ¼" (0.7 cm) seam allowance:

- Appliqué pieces of assorted scraps
- 1 **A** piece of grass fabric #1
- 1 **B** piece of grass fabric #2
- 1 front of main fabric
- 1 back of main fabric
- 1 bottom of main fabric
- 2 linings of lining fabric
- 1 bottom lining of lining fabric

Cut out the following piece, which does not have a template, according to the measurement below (this measurement includes seam allowance):

Assorted scraps:

- Zipper charm: 1 ½" (4 cm) diameter circle

Sew using ¼" (0.7 cm) seam allowance, unless otherwise noted.

CONSTRUCTION STEPS

1. Appliqué the pieces to the front (refer to template for placement). Sew A and B together, then appliqué to the front.

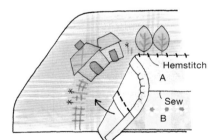

2. Working from the wrong side, trim the excess front fabric, leaving a ¼" (0.7 cm) seam allowance.

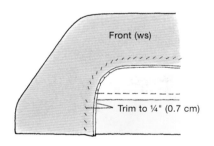

3. Align the front and lining with right sides together. Layer a piece of batting underneath. Sew, leaving an opening. Trim the excess batting from the seam allowance. Turn right side out.

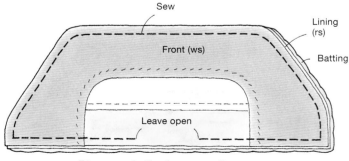

Trim excess batting from seam allowance

4. Hemstitch the opening closed. Quilt with ⅝" (1.5 cm) squares. Fold the zipper ends under and hemstitch one side of the zipper to the front (refer to template for placement). (**Note:** You may need to trim excess zipper length before sewing to the front.)

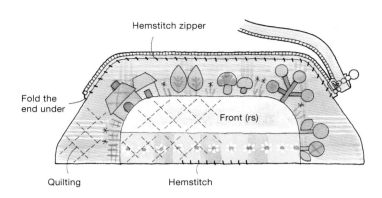

Hemstitch zipper

Fold the end under

Front (rs)

Quilting

Hemstitch

5. Follow the same process used in steps 3-4 to make and quilt the back, then hemstitch the other side of the zipper to the back.

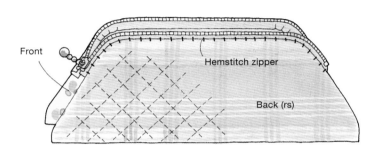

Front

Hemstitch zipper

Back (rs)

6. Align the bottom and lining with right sides together. Layer a piece of batting underneath. Sew, leaving an opening. Turn right side out and hemstitch the opening closed. Quilt with ⅝" (1.5 cm) squares.

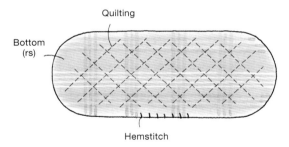

Quilting

Bottom (rs)

Hemstitch

8. Make the zipper charm (refer to page 12).

7. Whipstitch the front and back together along the sides, stitching through the top fabric only (refer to page 11). With right sides together, align the bottom and whipstitch to the pouch, stitching through the top fabric only once again.

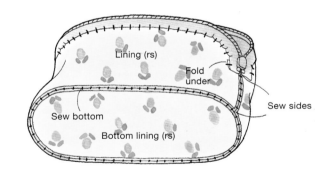

Lining (rs)

Fold under

Sew bottom

Bottom lining (rs)

Sew sides

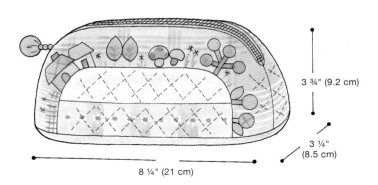

3 ¾" (9.2 cm)

3 ¼" (8.5 cm)

8 ¼" (21 cm)

12 Irish Chain Tote

I started making this bag while teaching a class on the traditional Irish Chain quilting pattern, but once I began sewing the little fabric squares together, this project evolved into something completely different. This bag is constructed using a unique windmill-inspired method. Once you master the technique, you can apply the same principles to construct bags featuring a variety of different quilt blocks.

A wide gusset allows you to store a lot in this bag.

MATERIALS

- **Patchwork fabric:** Assorted scraps
- **Main fabric:** ½ yard of pink fabric
- **Lining fabric:** ⅝ yard of print fabric
- **Batting:** 21 ¾" x 31 ½" (55 x 80 cm)
- One set of 19" (48 cm) handles
- One 1 ¼" (3 cm) diameter cover button

PATCHWORK DIAGRAM

BAG

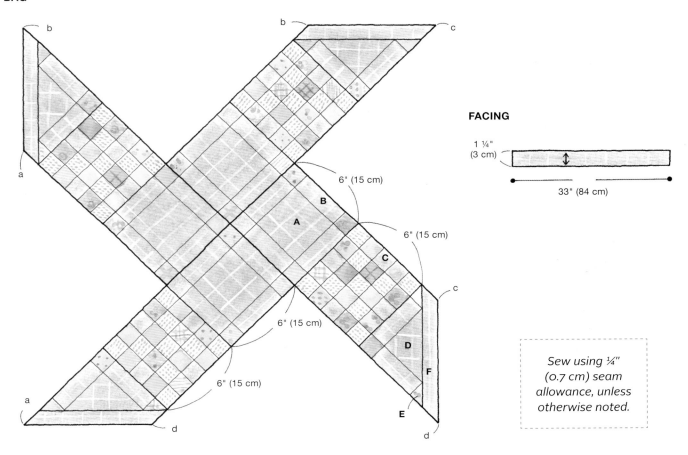

FACING

1 ¼"
(3 cm)

33" (84 cm)

*Sew using ¼"
(0.7 cm) seam
allowance, unless
otherwise noted.*

CUTTING INSTRUCTIONS

Trace and cut out the templates on page 125 (refer to page 6 for instructions on using templates). Cut the following fabric pieces adding ¼" (0.7 cm) seam allowance:

- 104 **C** pieces of assorted scraps
- 8 **E** pieces of assorted scraps
- 4 **A** pieces of main fabric
- 24 **B** pieces of main fabric
- 16 **C** pieces of main fabric
- 4 **D** pieces of main fabric
- 4 **F** pieces of main fabric

Cut out the following pieces, which do not have templates, according to the measurements below (these measurements include seam allowance):

Assorted scraps:
- Covered button: 1 ¾" (4.5 cm) diameter circle

Main fabric:
- Facing: 1 ¾" x 33 ½" (4.4 x 85.4 cm)

CONSTRUCTION STEPS

1. Sew pieces A-F together to make one patchwork panel. Cut out a lining in the shape of the completed patchwork panel, adding ½" (1.2 cm) extra seam allowance on the long side only. Layer the patchwork panel, batting, and lining. Quilt as shown in the diagram below. Repeat process to make and quilt three more patchwork panels.

2. Sew the four patchwork panels together following the layout shown in the diagram below. With right sides together, match the a, b, c, and d points and sew into a bag shape, using the technique shown on page 11 to sew the bag together and finish the seam allowances using the lining. Make the covered button (refer to page 12) and hemstitch to the center bottom seam allowance inside the bag.

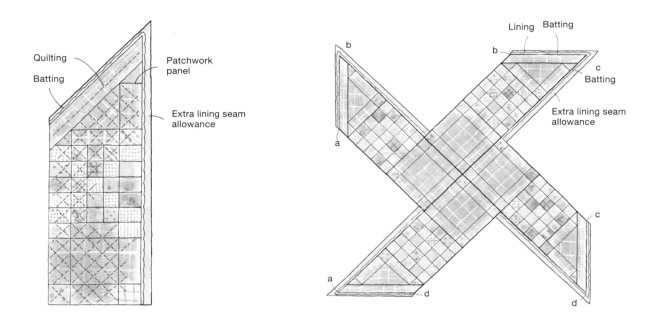

3. With right sides together, sew the two short ends of the facing together. Next, sew the facing to the bag opening with right sides together. Turn the facing right side out and fold to bring the facing to the inside of the bag. Hemstitch the facing to the lining. Backstitch the handles to the bag using two strands of quilting thread (refer to the diagram below for placement).

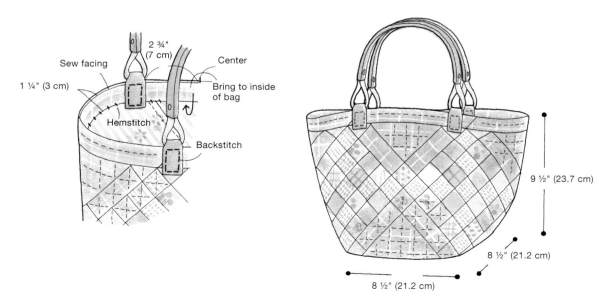

13 Modern Quilter's Bag

This unique bag combines traditional yarn-dyed fabric with frame-shaped appliqué motifs to create a modern design. I added a few flower motifs to provide contrast to the geometric shapes.

MATERIALS

- **Appliqué fabric:** Assorted scraps
- **Main fabric:** ⅝ yard of gray fabric
- **Lining fabric:** ½ yard of print fabric
- **Batting:** 17 ¾" x 39 ½" (45 x 100 cm)
- One set of 16" (41 cm) handles
- No. 25 embroidery floss in green, white, and red

PATCHWORK DIAGRAM

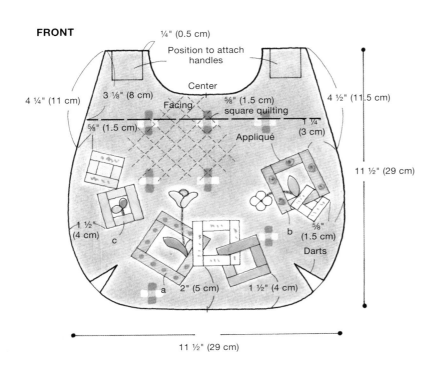

FRONT

- ¼" (0.5 cm)
- Position to attach handles
- Center
- 3 ⅛" (8 cm)
- Facing
- ⅝" (1.5 cm) square quilting
- 4 ½" (11.5 cm)
- 4 ¼" (11 cm)
- ⅝" (1.5 cm)
- ¼" (3 cm)
- Appliqué
- 11 ½" (29 cm)
- 1 ½" (4 cm)
- c
- b
- ⅝" (1.5 cm)
- Darts
- a
- 2" (5 cm)
- 1 ½" (4 cm)
- 11 ½" (29 cm)

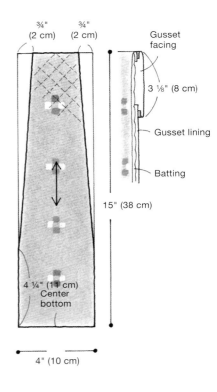

GUSSET

- ¾" (2 cm)
- ¾" (2 cm)
- Gusset facing
- 3 ⅛" (8 cm)
- Gusset lining
- Batting
- 15" (38 cm)
- 4 ¼" (11 cm)
- Center bottom
- 4" (10 cm)

CUTTING INSTRUCTIONS

Trace and cut out the templates on Pattern Sheet B (refer to page 6 for instructions on using templates). Cut the following fabric pieces adding ¼" (0.7 cm) seam allowance:

- Front/back (cut 1 of each) of main fabric
- Appliqué pieces of assorted scraps
- 2 facings of main fabric
- 2 linings of lining fabric

Cut out the following pieces, which do not have templates, according to the measurements on the right (these measurements include seam allowance):

Main fabric:
- Gusset (cut 2): 4 ½" x 15 ½" (11.4 x 39.4 cm)
- Gusset facing (cut 2): 3 ⅝" x 4 ½" (9.4 x 11.4 cm)

Lining fabric:
- Gusset lining (cut 2): 4 ½" x 12 ¼" (11.4 x 31.4 cm)

BACK

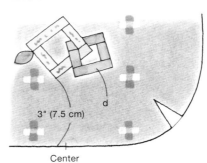

- d
- 3" (7.5 cm)
- Center

Sew using ¼" (0.7 cm) seam allowance, unless otherwise noted.

CONSTRUCTION STEPS

1. Appliqué the motifs to the bag front and back following the numerical order listed in the diagram below (refer to the diagrams on page 58 for placement). Embroider as indicated on the templates.

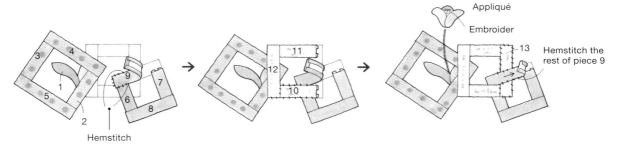

2. With right sides together, sew a facing to each lining. Align the assembled lining and front with right sides together. Layer a piece of batting underneath. Sew, leaving an opening. Make clips in the curved sections of the seam allowance. Turn right side out and quilt as shown in the diagram on page 58. Sew the darts and hemstitch the seam allowances to the lining. Repeat the process for the back.

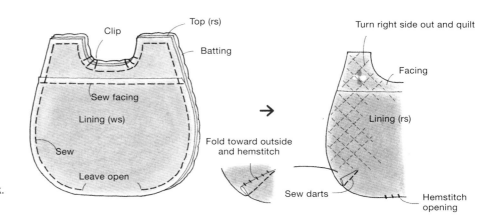

3. With right sides together, sew the two gussets together along the center bottom. With right sides together, sew the two gusset linings together along the center bottom. With right sides together, sew a gusset facing to each short end of the gusset lining. Trim both sides of the gusset and gusset lining so the pieces taper in ¾" (2 cm) starting 4 ¼" (11 cm) from the center. With right sides together, layer the gusset, gusset lining, and batting. Sew, leaving an opening. Turn right side out and quilt with ⅝" (1.5 cm) squares. With right sides together, whipstitch the gusset to the front and back, stitching through the top fabric only (refer to page 11). Backstitch the handles to the bag using two strands of quilting thread (refer to the diagram on page 58 for placement).

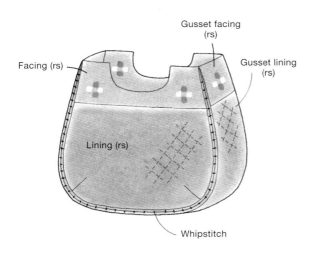

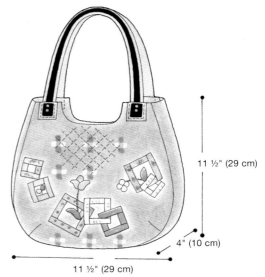

14 Double Wedding Ring Tote

This tote bag offers a modern interpretation of the traditional Double Wedding Ring quilt pattern. The neutral background fabric, bold print fabrics, and red handle combine to create a stylish, sophisticated bag.

MATERIALS

- **Patchwork and appliqué fabric:** Assorted scraps
- **Main fabric:** 1 yard of dark brown fabric
- **Accent fabric:** ⅓ yard of brown fabric
- **Lining fabric:** 1 yard of print fabric
- **Batting:** 17 ¾" x 27 ½" (45 x 70 cm)
- One 10" (25.5 cm) zipper
- One set of 19" (48 cm) handles

PATCHWORK DIAGRAM

BAG

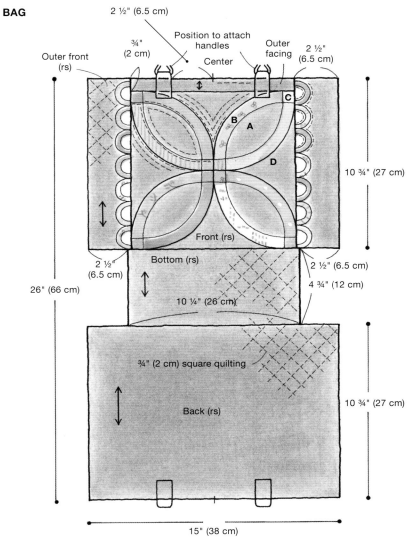

INNER FACING

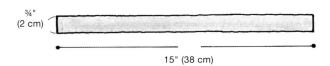

¾"
(2 cm)

15" (38 cm)

CUTTING INSTRUCTIONS

Trace and cut out the templates on Pattern Sheet B (refer to page 6 for instructions on using templates). Cut the following fabric pieces adding ¼" (0.7 cm) seam allowance:

- 4 **A** pieces of main fabric
- 8 **B** pieces of assorted scraps
- 8 **C** pieces of assorted scraps
- 4 **D** pieces of main fabric

Cut out the following pieces, which do not have templates, according to the measurements below (these measurements include seam allowance):

Main fabric:

- Outer fronts (cut 2): 3" x 11 ¼" (7.9 x 28.4 cm)
- Back: 11 ¼" x 15 ½" (28.4 x 39.4 cm)
- Outer facing: 1 ¼" x 10 ½" (3.4 x 26.4 cm)
- Inner facings (cut 2): 1 ¼" x 15 ½" (3.4 x 39.4 cm)

Accent fabric:

- Bottom: 5 ¼" x 10 ¾" (13.4 x 27.4 cm)

Lining fabric:

- Inside pocket: 10" x 14" (25.4 x 35.4 cm)
- Binding strips (cut lengthwise) ½ yard (0.5 m) of 1 ½" (3.5 cm) wide bias strips

Assorted scraps:

- Bias strips: 1 ½" x 3 ½" (3.5 x 9 cm) bias strips

Sew using ¼" (0.7 cm) seam allowance, unless otherwise noted.

CONSTRUCTION STEPS

1. Sew pieces A–D together to make the patchwork panel. Sew the outer facing to the top of the patchwork panel. Fold the bias strips into ¼" x 3 ½" (0.7 x 9 cm) long pieces. Baste, then appliqué to the outer fronts using the template to form the pieces into a curved shape. Sew an appliquéd outer front to each side of the patchwork panel. Sew the front, bottom, and back together following the placement indicated in the diagram on page 61.

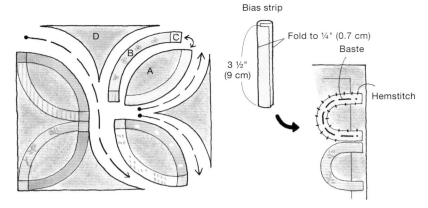

2. Cut the lining in the shape of the completed top, adding ½" (1.2 cm) extra seam allowance along each side. Layer the top, batting, and lining. Quilt as shown in the diagram on page 61. Fold the bag in half with right sides together. Use the technique shown on page 16 to sew the front and back together along the sides and finish the seam allowances using the lining.

3. Align each side seam with the bottom fold. Miter each corner and bind the seam allowances using the binding strips. Refer to steps 5 and 6 on pages 28-29 to make the inside pocket.

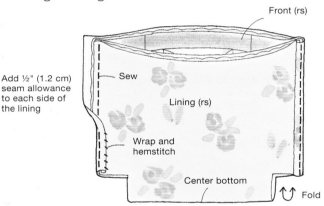

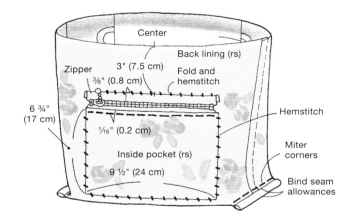

Refer to page 11 for instructions on finishing the seam allowances using lining.

4. With right sides together, sew the short ends of the inner facings together. With right sides together, sew the inner facing to the bag opening. Turn the facing right side out and fold to bring the facing to the inside of the bag. Hemstitch the facing to the lining. Backstitch the handles to the bag using two strands of quilting thread (refer to the diagram on page 61 for placement).

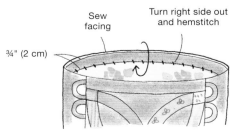

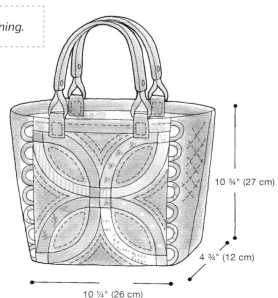

Embellished Patch Tote

As much as I love color, I have recently started to appreciate gray for its beauty and elegance. Believe it or not, the bag and appliqué patches are made with the same fabric—I used the reverse side of the gray yarn-dyed fabric to create the white patches. This bag looks great when paired with a white outfit or pearl jewelry.

MATERIALS

- **Main fabric:** ½ yard of gray yarn-dyed fabric
- **Lining fabric:** ⅝ yard of print fabric
- **Batting:** 17 ¾" x 25 ½" (45 x 65 cm)
- **Four 1" (2.5 cm) diameter cover buttons**
- **One set of 13" (33 cm) handles**
- **No. 5 pearl cotton in white and green**

PATCHWORK DIAGRAM

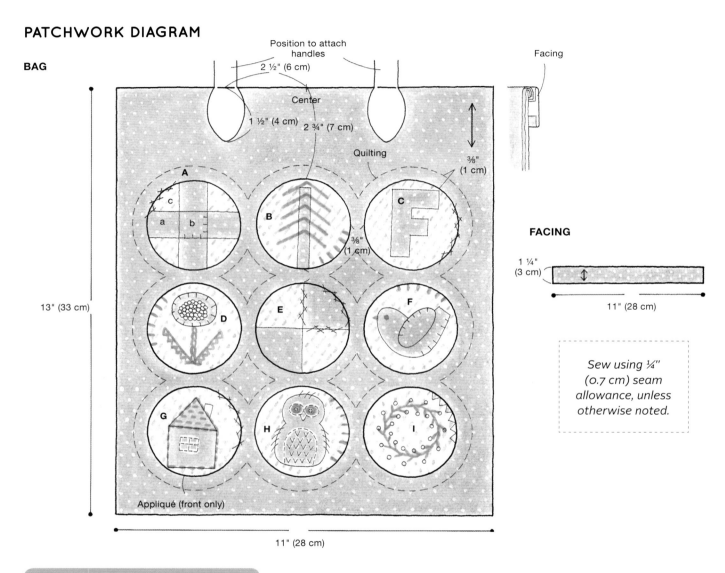

Sew using ¼" (0.7 cm) seam allowance, unless otherwise noted.

CUTTING INSTRUCTIONS

Trace and cut out the templates on page 126 (refer to page 6 for instructions on using templates). Cut the following fabric pieces adding ¼" (0.7 cm) seam allowance:

- Appliqué pieces of main fabric

Cut out the following pieces, which do not have templates, according to the measurements on the right (these measurements include seam allowance):

Main fabric:
- Front/back (cut 1 of each): 11 ½" x 13 ½" (29.4 x 34.4 cm)
- Facing (cut 2): 1 ¾" x 11 ½" (4.4 x 29.4 cm)

Lining fabric:
- Front/back lining (cut 1 of each): 12 ½" x 14" (32 x 35.7 cm)
- Inside pocket: 9 ¼" x 16 ½" (23.4 x 42.4 cm)
- Covered buttons (cut 4): 1 ½" (4 cm) diameter circles

CONSTRUCTION STEPS

1. Appliqué the patches to the front and embroider as indicated on the templates and in the key at right. Layer the front, batting, and lining so the pieces are aligned at the top. (**Note:** The lining will be larger along the sides and bottom.) Quilt as shown in the diagram on page 64. Next, layer the back, batting, and lining. Quilt as desired.

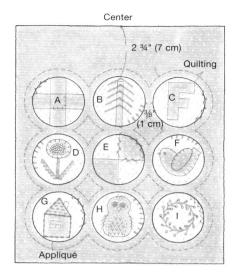

Center

2 ¾" (7 cm)

Quilting

⅜" (1 cm)

Appliqué

Patch	Stitches	Color
A	• Blanket • Outline • Herringbone	White
B	• Blanket	Green
C	• Outline • Herringbone	White
D	• Blanket	Green
E	• Herringbone	White
F	• Blanket	Green & White
G	• Outline • Herringbone	Green & White
H	• Blanket	Green
I	• Fly	White

2. Fold the inside pocket in half with right sides together and sew around three sides, leaving an opening. Turn right side out and hemstitch the opening closed.

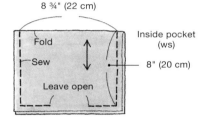

8 ¾" (22 cm)

Fold

Sew

Leave open

Inside pocket (ws)

8" (20 cm)

3. Use the technique shown on page 16 to sew the front and back together along the sides and bottom and finish the seam allowances using the lining. With right sides together, sew the short ends of the facings together. Sew the facing to the bag opening with right sides together. Turn the facing right side out and fold to bring the facing to the inside of the bag. Hemstitch the facing to the lining. Hemstitch the inside pocket to the bag lining, about 3 ⅛" (8 cm) below the facing. Backstitch the handles to the bag using two strands of quilting thread (refer to the diagram on page 64 for placement). Make the covered buttons (refer to page 12) and hemstitch to the bag lining to cover the stitching from the handles.

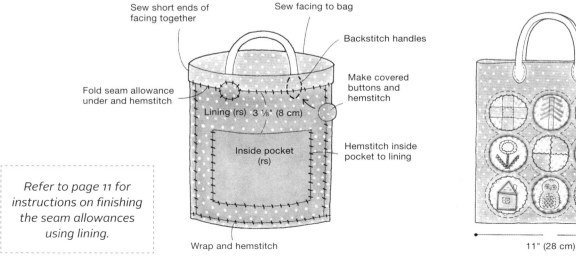

Sew short ends of facing together

Sew facing to bag

Backstitch handles

Fold seam allowance under and hemstitch

Make covered buttons and hemstitch

Lining (rs)   3 ⅛" (8 cm)

Inside pocket (rs)

Hemstitch inside pocket to lining

Refer to page 11 for instructions on finishing the seam allowances using lining.

Wrap and hemstitch

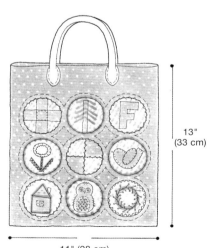

13" (33 cm)

11" (28 cm)

(16) Appliquéd Boston Bag

(17) Embroidered Eyeglass Case

Although this Boston bag is on the larger side, it is very lightweight and elegant. Fusible interfacing helps to stabilize the bag and allows it to maintain its unique shape. I designed this eyeglass case after a fruitless search for a ready-made, sophisticated case. This case is embellished with a Japanese beautyberry motif featuring a vibrant purple color scheme.

This case includes special lining made from shrinkable plastic, which will protect your glasses. You can also remove the lining and use the case as a little zippered pouch.

FRONT

BACK

Special details, including three-dimensional appliqué, embroidery, and yoyos, bring this bag to life.

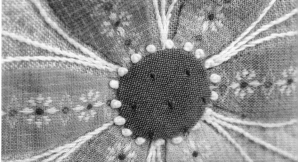

Appliquéd Boston Bag

MATERIALS

- **Appliqué fabric:** Assorted scraps
- **Main fabric:** ½ yard of beige fabric
- **Accent fabric:** ⅝ yard of light blue fabric
- **Lining fabric:** ⅝ yard of print fabric

- **Batting:** 23 ¾" x 31 ½" (60 x 80 cm)
- **Lightweight fusible interfacing:** 27 ½" x 35 ½" (70 x 90 cm)
- Two 11" (28 cm) zippers

- One set of 19" (48 cm) handles
- No. 25 embroidery floss in white
- Candlewicking floss in white
- Scraps of yarn

PATCHWORK DIAGRAM

FRONT & BACK

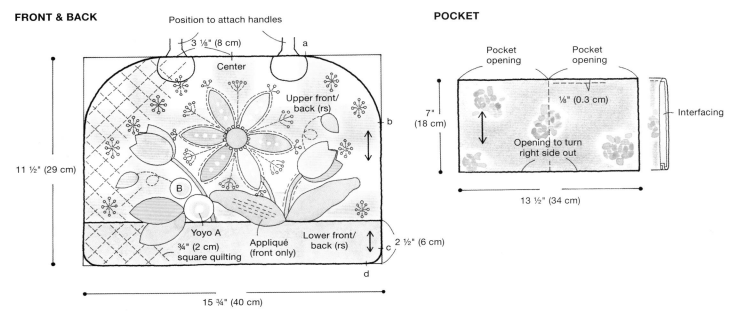

Position to attach handles

3 ⅛" (8 cm)
a
Center
Upper front/back (rs)
b
11 ½" (29 cm)
B
Yoyo A
¾" (2 cm) square quilting
Appliqué (front only)
Lower front/back (rs)
c
2 ½" (6 cm)
d
15 ¾" (40 cm)

POCKET

Pocket opening
Pocket opening
⅛" (0.3 cm)
7" (18 cm)
Opening to turn right side out
13 ½" (34 cm)
Interfacing

TOP GUSSET

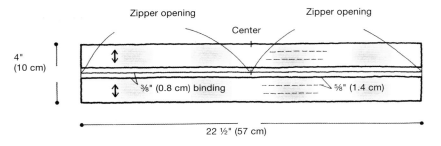

Zipper opening
Zipper opening
Center
4" (10 cm)
⅜" (0.8 cm) binding
⅝" (1.4 cm)
22 ½" (57 cm)

Sew using ¼" (0.7 cm) seam allowance, unless otherwise noted.

BOTTOM GUSSET

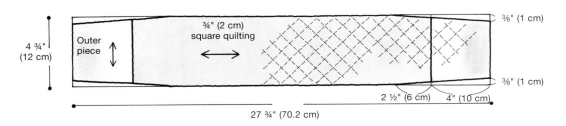

4 ¾" (12 cm)
Outer piece
¾" (2 cm) square quilting
⅜" (1 cm)
⅜" (1 cm)
2 ½" (6 cm)
4" (10 cm)
27 ¾" (70.2 cm)

Trace and cut out the templates on page 127-129 (refer to page 6 for instructions on using templates). Cut the following fabric pieces adding ¼" (0.7 cm) seam allowance:

- Appliqué pieces of assorted scraps

Cut out the following pieces, which do not have templates, according to the measurements below (these measurements include seam allowance):

Main fabric:
- Upper front/back (cut 1 of each): 9 ½" x 16 ¼" (24.4 x 41.4 cm)
- Top gusset (cut 2): 2 ¼" x 23" (5.6 x 58.4 cm)
- Bias strips: 1 ½ yards (1.5 m) of 1 ½" (3.5 cm) wide bias strips
- Outer pieces (cut 2): 4 ½" x 5 ¼" (11.4 x 13.4 cm)

Accent fabric:
- Lower front/back (cut 1 of each): 3" x 16 ¼" (7.4 x 41.4 cm)
- Bottom gusset: 5 ¼" x 20 ¼" (13.4 x 51.6 cm)

Lining fabric:
- Front/back lining (cut 1 of each): 12" x 16 ¼" (30.4 x 41.4 cm)
- Top gusset lining (cut 2): 2 ¾" x 23" (6.9 x 58.4 cm)
- Bottom gusset lining: 6 ¼" x 28 ¼" (16 x 71.6 cm)
- Pocket: 14" x 14 ½" (35.4 x 37.4 cm)

Fusible interfacing:
- Front/back interfacing (cut 1 of each): 12" x 16 ¼" (30.4 x 41.4 cm)
- Top gusset interfacing (cut 2): 2 ¼" x 23" (5.6 x 58.4 cm)
- Bottom gusset interfacing: 5 ¼" x 28 ¼" (13.4 x 71.6 cm)
- Pocket interfacing: 7" x 13 ½" (18 x 34 cm)

Assorted scraps:
- Yoyo A: 1 ¼" x 5 ½" (3 x 14 cm)
- Yoyo B: ¾" x 4 ¾" (2 x 12 cm)
- Zipper charm (cut 2): 1 ½" x 2 ½" (3.5 x 6.5 cm)

CONSTRUCTION STEPS

1. Appliqué the flowers and stems to the upper front. Embroider the remaining stems as indicated on the templates. With right sides together, sew the lower sections to the front and back. Adhere fusible interfacing to the wrong sides of the front and back. Use the curve template on page 129 to cut the front and back into a rounded shape.

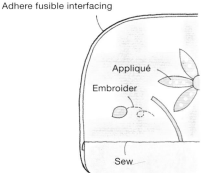

Adhere fusible interfacing

Appliqué

Embroider

Sew

2. For both the front and back, layer the top, batting, and lining. Quilt as shown in the diagram on page 68. Finish embroidering the front as indicated on the templates.

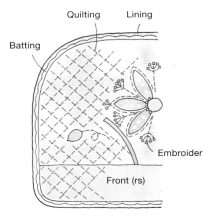

Quilting   Lining

Batting

Embroider

Front (rs)

3. Align two large leaf pieces with right sides together. Layer on top of a piece of batting cut out in the shape of the leaf. Sew, leaving an opening. Make clips in the curved sections of the seam allowance. Turn right side out and hemstitch the opening closed. Quilt as indicated on the template. Use a needle to insert pieces of yarn into the channels created by the quilting. Trim excess yarn close to the fabric and gently stretch the fabric to make the yarn ends disappear. Use the same process to make another symmetrical large leaf.

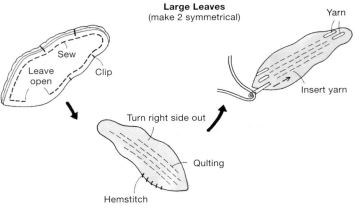

Large Leaves
(make 2 symmetrical)

Sew

Leave open

Clip

Yarn

Insert yarn

Turn right side out

Qulting

Hemstitch

4. Follow the same process used in step 3 to make two small leaves and four flowers.

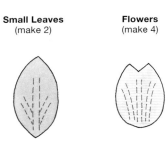

Small Leaves
(make 2)

Flowers
(make 4)

5. To make Yoyo A, fold the fabric in half with right sides together. Sew the two short ends together. Turn right side out. Fray the bottom edge for ¼" (0.7 cm). Fold the top seam allowance over ¼" (0.5 cm). Running stitch in the seam allowance, leaving long thread tails. Pull the thread tails to gather the fabric into a circle. Use the same process to make Yoyo B.

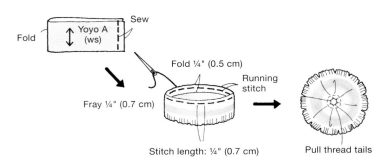

Fold

Yoyo A
(ws)

Sew

Fold ¼" (0.5 cm)

Running stitch

Fray ¼" (0.7 cm)

Stitch length: ¼" (0.7 cm)

Pull thread tails

6. Appliqué the flowers, leaves, and yoyos to the bag front, making sure to leave the top portions unattached as shown in the diagram below.

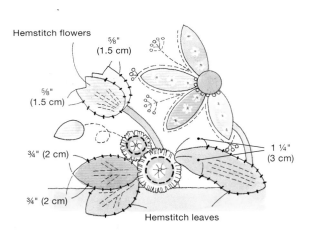

Hemstitch flowers

⅝"
(1.5 cm)

⅝"
(1.5 cm)

¾" (2 cm)

1 ¼"
(3 cm)

¾" (2 cm)

Hemstitch leaves

7. Adhere fusible interfacing to the wrong side of each top gusset. Layer each top gusset, batting and lining so the pieces are aligned along one long edge. (**Note:** The lining will be larger along the other long edge.) Quilt as shown in the diagram on page 68. Use the bias strips to bind the long edge of each quilted gusset where the pieces are aligned. Sew the two zippers to the bindings so that the zipper pulls meet in the center.

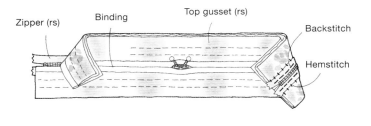

Zipper (rs)

Binding

Top gusset (rs)

Backstitch

Hemstitch

8. With right sides together, sew an outer piece to each short end of the bottom gusset. Adhere fusible interfacing to the wrong side of the assembled bottom gusset. Pin the bottom gusset and batting together and trim so the pieces taper in ⅜" (1 cm) on each side, starting 6 ¾" (16.5 cm) from the end. Unpin the layers. Using the bottom gusset as a template, trim the gusset lining into a tapered shape, leaving ½" (1.2 cm) extra seam allowance on each long edge. With right sides together, align the bottom and top gussets. Layer the bottom gusset lining and batting underneath. Sew along each short end.

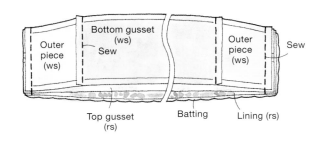

Outer piece
(ws)

Bottom gusset
(ws)
Sew

Outer piece
(ws)

Sew

Top gusset
(rs)

Batting

Lining (rs)

9. Turn the assembled gusset right side out. Quilt the bottom gusset with ¾" (2 cm) squares.

10. Use the technique shown on page 11 to sew the gusset to the bag front and back and finish the seam allowances using the lining. (**Note:** The gusset lining seam allowances will be larger.)

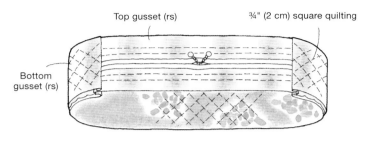

Top gusset (rs)

¾" (2 cm) square quilting

Bottom gusset (rs)

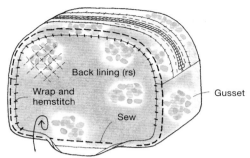

Back lining (rs)

Wrap and hemstitch

Sew

Gusset

11. With right sides together, fold the pocket in half. Adhere fusible interfacing to the wrong side of one half. Sew around the sides and bottom, leaving an opening. Turn right side out and hemstitch the opening closed. Topstitch along the top of the pocket. Hemstitch the pocket to the inside of the bag. Backstitch along the center of the pocket, making sure to stitch through the bag lining only so the stitches won't be visible on the bag outside.

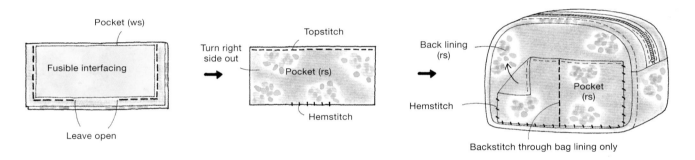

Pocket (ws)

Fusible interfacing

Leave open

Turn right side out

Topstitch

Pocket (rs)

Hemstitch

Back lining (rs)

Hemstitch

Pocket (rs)

Backstitch through bag lining only

12. Fold each zipper charm piece in half with right sides together. Sew the short ends together, then turn right side out. Fold the top and bottom edges over ¼" (0.5 cm). Running stitch in the seam allowance, leaving long thread tails. Position each zipper charm over a zipper pull. Insert a small scrap of batting. Pull the thread tails to gather the fabric around the zipper pull. Secure the thread ends. Backstitch the handles to the bag using two strands of quilting thread (refer to the diagram on page 68 for placement).

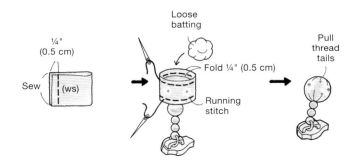

¼" (0.5 cm)

Sew

(ws)

Loose batting

Fold ¼" (0.5 cm)

Running stitch

Pull thread tails

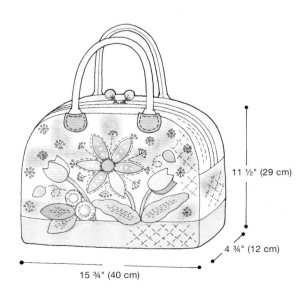

11 ½" (29 cm)

4 ¾" (12 cm)

15 ¾" (40 cm)

Embroidered Eyeglass Case

MATERIALS

- **Appliqué fabric:** Assorted scraps
- **Main fabric:** ⅛ yard of beige fabric
- **Accent fabric:** ⅛ yard of striped fabric
- **Binding fabric:** One 1 ½" x 27 ½" (3.5 x 70 cm) bias strip

- **Lining fabric:** ⅓ yard of print fabric
- **Batting:** 9 ¾" x 9 ¾" (25 x 25 cm)
- **Lightweight fusible interfacing:** 6" x 6" (15 x 15 cm)
- One 10" (25.5 cm) zipper

- 6" x 6" (15 x 15 cm) of shrinkable plastic
- No. 25 embroidery floss in purple, green, and brown
- No. 5 pearl cotton in beige

PATCHWORK DIAGRAM

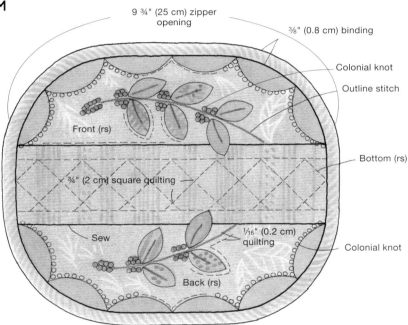

9 ¾" (25 cm) zipper opening

⅜" (0.8 cm) binding

Colonial knot

Outline stitch

Front (rs)

Bottom (rs)

¾" (2 cm) square quilting

Sew

1/16" (0.2 cm) quilting

Colonial knot

Back (rs)

Sew using ¼" (0.7 cm) seam allowance, unless otherwise noted.

CUTTING INSTRUCTIONS

Trace and cut out the templates on page 130 (refer to page 6 for instructions on using templates). Cut the following fabric pieces adding ¼" (0.7 cm) seam allowance:

- 1 inner case of main fabric
- 1 inner case of lining fabric
- 1 inner case of fusible interfacing
- 1 bottom of accent fabric
- 1 front of main fabric
- 1 back of main fabric

- Appliqué pieces of assorted scraps
- 1 zipper charm of assorted scraps

Cut out the following pieces, which do not have templates, according to the measurement below (this measurement includes seam allowance):

Binding fabric:
- Bias strips: One 1 ½" x 27 ½" (3.5 x 70 cm) bias strip

CONSTRUCTION STEPS

1. Adhere fusible interfacing to the wrong side of the inner case lining. Align the inner case and lining with right sides together. Layer a piece of batting on top. Sew together around three sides, leaving one short side open.

2. Turn right side out. Fold the seam allowances along the open edge and press. Topstitch to divide the inner case into three sections (refer to the dotted line on template for placement). Cut pieces of plastic ⅛" (0.3 cm) smaller than each section and insert into the inner case underneath the batting.

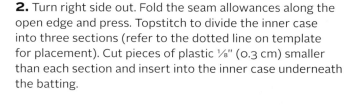

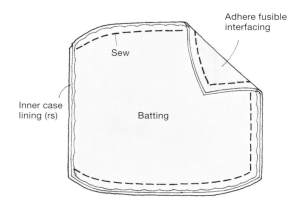

Adhere fusible interfacing

Sew

Inner case lining (rs)

Batting

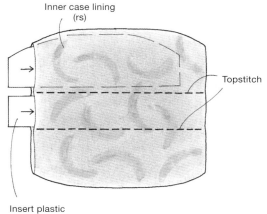

Inner case lining (rs)

Topstitch

Insert plastic

3. Fold the inner case into shape so the side with the batting is positioned on the inside. This will cushion the glasses while they are inside the case. Hemstitch the opening closed.

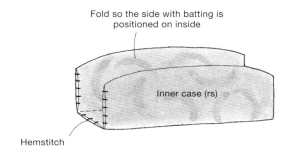

Fold so the side with batting is positioned on inside

Inner case (rs)

Hemstitch

4. With right sides together, sew the bottom to both the front and back. Appliqué and embroider the front and back as indicated on the template. Cut out a lining in the shape of the assembled top. Layer the top, batting, and lining. Quilt as indicated in the diagram on page 72. Use the bias strip to bind the edges. Fold the case in half with right sides together. Sew the zipper to binding as shown below. Whipstitch the bindings together at each end of the zipper. Align each side with the bottom fold. Miter each corner by sewing a 1 ¼" (3 cm) long seam. Turn the case right side out. Make the zipper charm (refer to page 12).

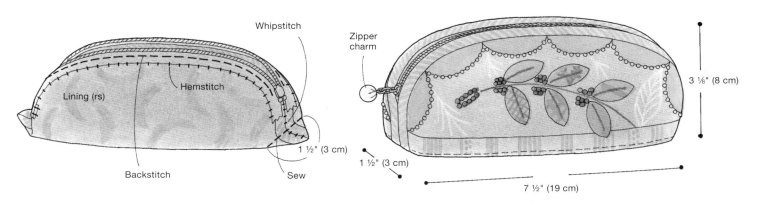

Whipstitch

Hemstitch

Lining (rs)

Backstitch

Sew

1 ½" (3 cm)

Zipper charm

1 ½" (3 cm)

3 ⅛" (8 cm)

7 ½" (19 cm)

18 Hawaiian Carryall

In my opinion, white is the epitome of elegance. I chose a white and beige color scheme for this Hawaiian-inspired tote bag. Try brighter colors, such as blue, pink, or mint green for a festive, summery bag.

MATERIALS

- **Appliqué fabric:** ⅝ yard of white fabric
- **Main fabric:** ¾ yard of beige fabric
- **Lining fabric:** 1 yard of print fabric
- **Batting:** 21 ¾" x 33 ½" (55 x 85 cm)
- One 9" (23 cm) zipper
- One set of 19" (48 cm) handles

PATCHWORK DIAGRAM

*Sew using ¼"
(0.7 cm) seam
allowance, unless
otherwise noted.*

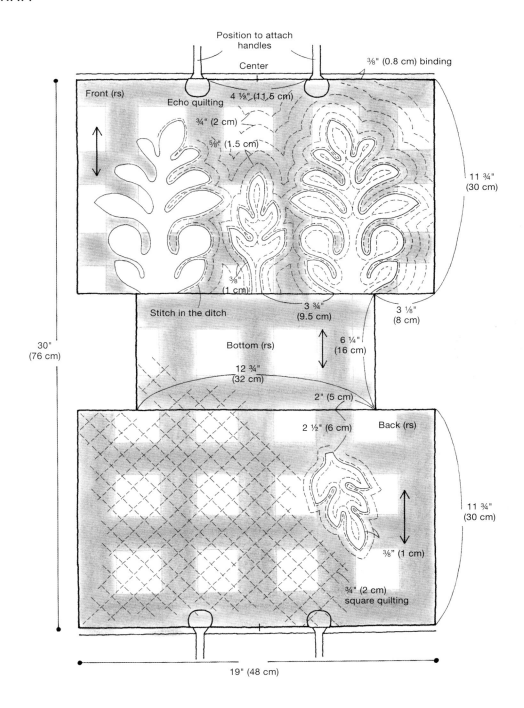

Position to attach
handles

Center

⅜" (0.8 cm) binding

Front (rs)

Echo quilting

4 ½" (11.5 cm)

¾" (2 cm)

⅝" (1.5 cm)

11 ¾"
(30 cm)

30"
(76 cm)

Stitch in the ditch

⅜"
(1 cm)

3 ¾"
(9.5 cm)

3 ⅛"
(8 cm)

Bottom (rs)

6 ¼"
(16 cm)

12 ¾"
(32 cm)

2" (5 cm)

2 ½" (6 cm)

Back (rs)

11 ¾"
(30 cm)

⅜" (1 cm)

¾" (2 cm)
square quilting

19" (48 cm)

CUTTING INSTRUCTIONS

Trace and cut out the templates on Pattern Sheet B (refer to page 6 for instructions on using templates). Cut the following fabric pieces:

- 2 small leaves of appliqué fabric
- 2 large leaves of appliqué fabric*

*The large leaves should be symmetrical. Use the right side of the large leaf template for the right leaf and the wrong side for the left leaf.

Cut out the following pieces, which do not have templates, according to the measurements on the right (these measurements include seam allowance):

Main fabric:
- Front/back (cut 1 of each): 12 ¼" x 19 ½" (31.4 x 49.4 cm)
- Bottom: 6 ¾" x 13 ¼" (17.4 x 33.4 cm)
- Binding strips (cut lengthwise): 1 ¼ yards (1.25 m) of 1 ½" (3.5 cm) wide strips

Lining fabric:
- Lining: 20 ½" x 30 ½" (52 x 77.4 cm)
- Inside pocket: 10" x 14" (25.4 x 35.4 cm)
- Binding strips (cut lengthwise): ½ yard (0.5 m) of 1 ½" (3.5 cm) wide strips

CONSTRUCTION STEPS

1. Baste the appliqué motifs to the bag front and back, stitching ½" (1.2 cm) from the raw edge (refer to the diagram on page 75 for placement).

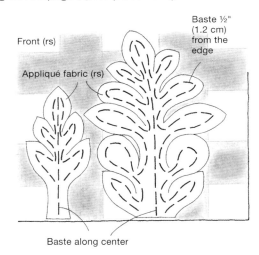

Front (rs)

Appliqué fabric (rs)

Baste ½" (1.2 cm) from the edge

Baste along center

2. Fold the seam allowances under and slipstitch the appliqué motifs in place.

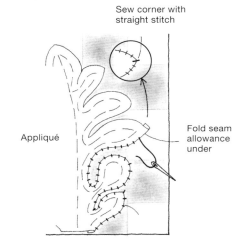

Sew corner with straight stitch

Appliqué

Fold seam allowance under

3. Sew the bottom to the bag front and back following the placement indicated in the diagram on page 75. Layer the assembled top, batting, and lining. (**Note:** The lining will be larger than the other pieces.) Quilt as shown in the diagram on page 75.

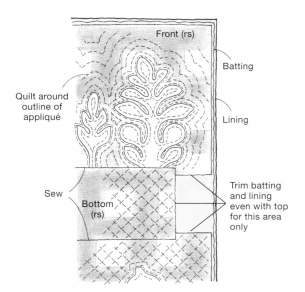

Front (rs)

Batting

Quilt around outline of appliqué

Lining

Sew

Bottom (rs)

Trim batting and lining even with top for this area only

4. Fold the inside pocket in half with right sides together and sew around three sides, leaving an opening. Turn right side out and hemstitch the opening closed. Sew one side of the zipper to the folded edge of the pocket. Fold the other side of the zipper in half and sew using 1/16" (0.2 cm) seam allowance.

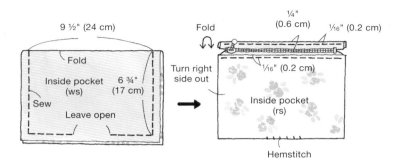

5. Fold the bag in half with right sides together. Use the technique shown on page 16 to sew the bag together along the sides and finish the seam allowances using the lining.

6. Align each side seam with the bottom fold. Miter each corner and bind the seam allowance using the lining binding strips. Hemstitch the pocket to the inside of the bag. Backstitch the other side of the zipper to the inside of the bag.

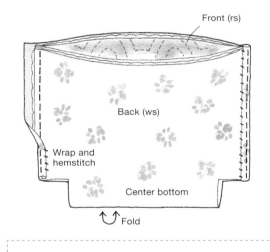

Refer to page 11 for instructions on finishing the seam allowances using lining.

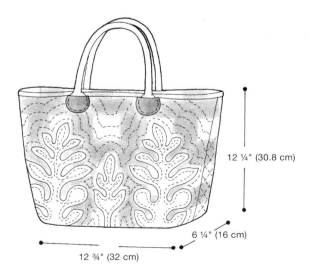

7. Use the main fabric binding strips to bind the bag opening. Backstitch the handles to the bag using two strands of quilting thread (refer to the diagram on page 75 for placement).

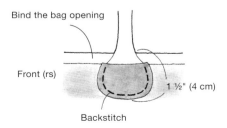

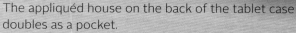
The appliquéd house on the back of the tablet case doubles as a pocket.

19 Village Tablet Case

20 House Pencil Case

Whenever I travel for workshops and classes, I always bring along my tablet and favorite pens. This matching tablet case and pencil case set helps me to stay organized and makes feel at home, no matter where in the world I may be!

Village Tablet Case

MATERIALS

- **Patchwork and appliqué fabric:** Assorted scraps
- **Main fabric:** ¾ yard of beige fabric
- **Lining fabric:** ½ yard of print fabric
- **Batting:** 8" x 23 ¾" (20 x 60 cm)

- **Fusible batting:** 4" x 21 ¾" (10 x 55 cm)
- **Lightweight fusible interfacing:** 5 ½" x 7" (14 x 18 cm)
- One 12" (30.5 cm) zipper
- One set of 15" (38 cm) handles

- No. 25 embroidery floss in brown, dark brown, green, and ocher
- No. 5 pearl cotton in ecru, brown, dark brown, red, and green

PATCHWORK DIAGRAM

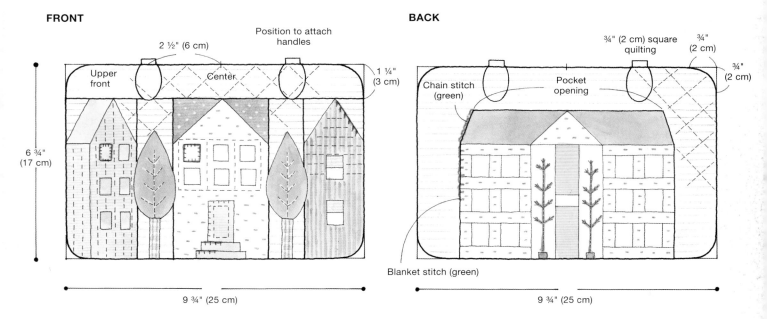

FRONT

2 ½" (6 cm)

Position to attach handles

Upper front

Center

1 ¼" (3 cm)

6 ¾" (17 cm)

9 ¾" (25 cm)

BACK

¾" (2 cm) square quilting

¾" (2 cm)

¾" (2 cm)

Chain stitch (green)

Pocket opening

Blanket stitch (green)

9 ¾" (25 cm)

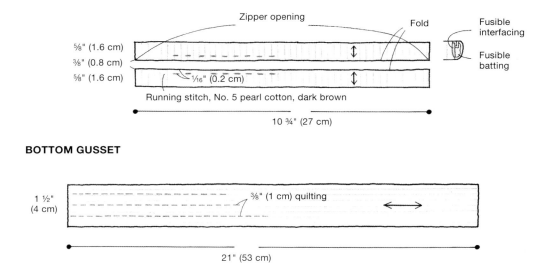

TOP GUSSETS

Zipper opening

Fold

Fusible interfacing

Fusible batting

⅝" (1.6 cm)

⅜" (0.8 cm)

⅝" (1.6 cm)

1/16" (0.2 cm)

Running stitch, No. 5 pearl cotton, dark brown

10 ¾" (27 cm)

BOTTOM GUSSET

1 ½" (4 cm)

⅜" (1 cm) quilting

21" (53 cm)

Sew using ¼" (0.7 cm) seam allowance, unless otherwise noted.

Note: When embroidering, use No. 25 embroidery floss, unless otherwise noted.

CUTTING INSTRUCTIONS

Trace and cut out the templates on pages 131-132 (refer to page 6 for instructions on using templates). Cut the following fabric pieces adding ¼" (0.7 cm) seam allowance:

- Patchwork pieces of assorted scraps and main fabric
- Appliqué pieces of assorted scraps
- Pocket lining of lining fabric

Cut out the following pieces, which do not have templates, according to the measurements below (these measurements include seam allowance):

Main fabric:

- Upper front: 1 ¾" x 10 ¼" (4.4 x 26.4 cm)
- Back: 7 ¼" x 10 ¼" (18.4 x 26.4 cm)
- Top gussets (cut 2): 1 ¾" x 11 ¼" (4.6 x 28.4 cm)
- Bottom gusset: 2" x 21 ½" (5.4 x 54.4 cm)

Lining fabric:

- Front lining: 7 ¼" x 10 ¼" (18.4 x 26.4 cm)
- Back lining: 7 ¼" x 10 ¼" (18.4 x 26.4 cm)
- Bottom gusset lining: 2" x 21 ½" (5.4 x 54.4 cm)

Fusible batting:

- Top gusset strips (cut 2): ⅝" x 10 ¾" (1.6 x 27 cm)
- Bottom gusset lining: 2" x 21 ½" (5.4 x 54.5 cm)

Fusible interfacing:

- Top gusset strips (cut 2): ⅝" x 10 ¾" (1.6 x 27 cm)
- Bottom gusset: 2" x 21 ½" (5.4 x 54.4 cm)

CONSTRUCTION STEPS

1. Sew the patchwork pieces and the upper front together to make the front (refer to the diagram on page 79 for layout). Appliqué the trees, windows, doors, and steps to the front (refer to the templates for placement).

2. Align the front and lining with right sides together. Layer a piece of batting underneath. Mark each side ¾" (2 cm) from the corner. Connect the marks with a curved line. Trim along the line to form the corners into a rounded shape. Sew around all four sides, leaving an opening.

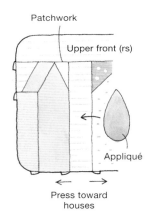

Patchwork

Upper front (rs)

Appliqué

Press toward houses

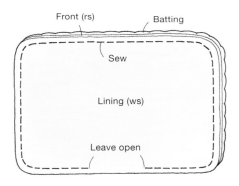

Front (rs)   Batting

Sew

Lining (ws)

Leave open

3. Trim the batting seam allowances and turn right side out. Hemstitch the opening closed. Quilt the front as shown in the diagram on page 79 and as indicated on the templates. Repeat step 2 for the bag back, then quilt with intersecting diagonal lines.

FRONT

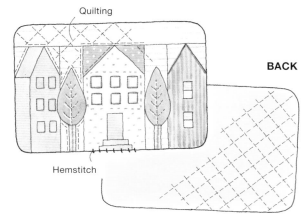

Quilting

BACK

Hemstitch

4. Sew the patchwork pieces together to create the house-shaped pocket (refer to the diagram on page 79 for layout). Adhere fusible interfacing to the wrong side of the pocket. Sew the pocket and lining with right sides together, leaving an opening.

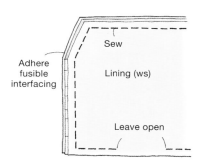

5. Turn the pocket right side out. Hemstitch the opening closed. Chain stitch along the roof line, then embroider the rest of the pocket as indicated on the template.

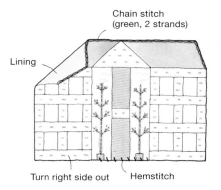

6. Hemstitch the pocket to the bag back, making sure to leave the pocket open along the top. Blanket stitch along the sides of the house.

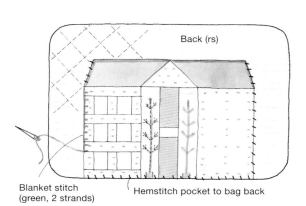

7. Adhere strips of fusible interfacing and fusible batting to the wrong side of each top gusset. Fold the seam allowance in on all sides, then fold each top gusset in half. Whipstitch together along each long edge. Embroider as shown in the diagram on page 79.

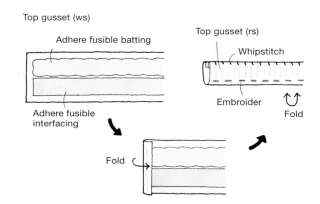

8. Adhere fusible interfacing to the wrong side of the bottom gusset and fusible batting to the wrong side of the bottom gusset lining. Sew the bottom gusset and lining with right sides together, leaving an opening. Turn right side out and hemstitch the opening closed. Quilt with horizontal lines about ⅜" (1 cm) apart.

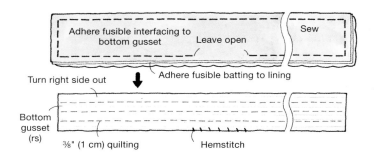

9. Whipstitch the top gussets to the bottom gusset to create a loop.

10. Backstitch the zipper to the top gusset linings. Fold the short ends of the zipper under and hemstitch to the gusset linings. Whipstitch the bag front and back to the assembled gusset (refer to page 11). Embroider the gusset with cross-stitch.

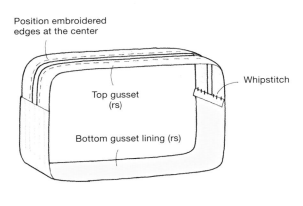

Position embroidered edges at the center

Top gusset (rs)

Bottom gusset lining (rs)

Whipstitch

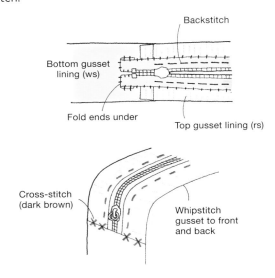

Backstitch

Bottom gusset lining (ws)

Fold ends under

Top gusset lining (rs)

Cross-stitch (dark brown)

Whipstitch gusset to front and back

11. To make the twisted cord, cut two 15 ¾" (40 cm) long strands each of No. 5 pearl cotton in green and brown. Tie the floss into two linked loops. Hold the brown loop in your left hand and the green loop in your right hand with the knots positioned at the center. Keep your left hand still while rotating your right hand about 80 times. Let the thread go slack and bring your hands together, which will cause the two colors of floss to twist around each other. To make the tassel, wrap brown No. 5 pearl cotton around a 4" (10 cm) wide piece of cardboard 20 times. Cut the loops and remove the floss from the cardboard. Align the twisted cord on top of the bundle of floss. Use a small piece of floss to tie a loop around the twisted cord and the bundle of floss. Fold the tassel in half. Wrap another small piece of floss around the top of the tassel a few times. Tie a knot and hide the ends inside the tassel. Attach the twisted cord tassel to the zipper pull. Backstitch the handles to the bag using two strands of quilting thread (refer to the diagram on page 79 for placement).

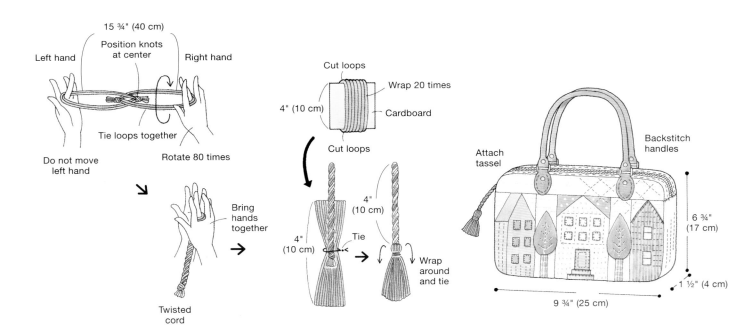

15 ¾" (40 cm)

Position knots at center

Left hand

Right hand

Do not move left hand

Tie loops together

Rotate 80 times

Bring hands together

Twisted cord

Cut loops

Wrap 20 times

4" (10 cm)

Cardboard

Cut loops

4" (10 cm)

4" (10 cm)

Tie

Wrap around and tie

Attach tassel

Backstitch handles

6 ¾" (17 cm)

1 ½" (4 cm)

9 ¾" (25 cm)

House Pencil Case

MATERIALS

- **Main fabric:** ¼ yard of beige fabric
- **Roof fabric:** ⅛ yard of blue fabric
- **Lining fabric:** ¼ yard of print fabric
- **Batting:** 4" x 15 ¾" (10 x 40 cm)
- One set of ¼" (0.5 cm) diameter snaps
- No. 25 embroidery floss in brown and light blue
- No. 5 pearl cotton in dark brown and green

CUTTING INSTRUCTIONS

Trace and cut out the templates on page 133 (refer to page 6 for instructions on using templates). Cut the following fabric pieces adding ¼" (0.7 cm) seam allowance:

- Roof flap patchwork pieces of roof fabric and main fabric

Cut out the following pieces, which do not have templates, according to the measurements

below (these measurements include seam allowance):

Main fabric:
- Pencil case: 2 ½" x 13 ¼" (6.4 x 33.4 cm)

Lining fabric:
- Pencil case lining: 2 ½" x 15 ¼" (6.4 x 38.4 cm)

PATCHWORK DIAGRAM

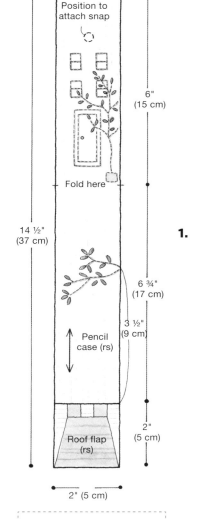

Sew using ¼" (0.7 cm) seam allowance, unless otherwise noted.

CONSTRUCTION STEPS

1. Sew the patchwork pieces together to create the roof flap. Sew the roof flap to the bottom of the pencil case. Embroider as indicated on the templates. Align the lining and assembled top with right sides together. Layer a piece of batting underneath. Sew around all four sides, leaving an opening.

2. Trim the batting seam allowances and turn right side out. Hemstitch the opening closed. Fold the pencil case 6" (15 cm) from the top. Whipstitch the sides of the pencil case together. Attach the snap components.

3. Refer to step 11 on page 82 to make a tassel using the dimensions indicated in the diagram below. Blanket stitch around the tassel cord.

4. Sew the tassel to the pencil case. Blanket stitch around the seams of the pencil case using brown No. 5 pearl cotton.

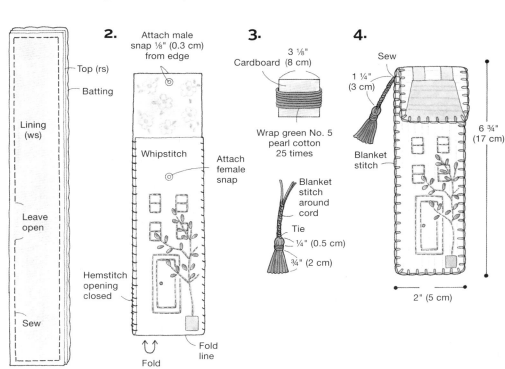

21 Bluebird Basket
22 Bluebird Tea Mat

I also bring this cute tea set with me whenever I travel. It is one of the first things I unpack when I check into my hotel room. After a long day of business meetings, it's important to have these little comforts of home waiting for me.

A stuffed bluebird hides under the roof of the basket!

Bluebird Basket

MATERIALS

- **Appliqué fabric:** Assorted scraps
- **Main fabric:** ⅓ yard of beige fabric
- **Roof fabric:** ¼ yard of brown fabric
- **Bird fabric:** ⅛ yard of light blue fabric
- **Lining fabric:** ½ yard of print fabric

- **Batting:** 13 ¾" x 13 ¾" (35 x 35 cm)
- Six ⅝" (1.5 cm) diameter cover buttons
- Handful of stuffing pellets
- No. 25 embroidery floss in green, mint, ocher, dark brown, and yellow green

- No. 5 pearl cotton in pink, light blue, and brown
- Candlewicking floss in variegated brown

CUTTING INSTRUCTIONS

Trace and cut out the templates on Pattern Sheet B (refer to page 6 for instructions on using templates). Cut the following fabric pieces adding ¼" (0.7 cm) seam allowance:

- 1 roof of roof fabric
- 1 roof of lining fabric
- 2 birds of bird fabric*
- 1 house of main fabric

- 1 house of lining fabric
- 1 bottom of main fabric
- 1 bottom of lining fabric

*The birds should be symmetrical. Use the right side of the template for one bird and the wrong side of the template for the other.

Cut out the following pieces, which do not have templates, according to the measurement below (this measurement includes seam allowance):

Assorted scraps:

- Covered buttons (cut 6): 1 ¼" (3 cm) diameter circles

CONSTRUCTION STEPS

Sew using ¼" (0.7 cm) seam allowance, unless otherwise noted.

1. Align the roof and lining with right sides together. Layer a piece of batting underneath. Sew together, leaving an opening. Trim the batting seam allowances and turn right side out. Hemstitch the opening closed. Quilt with intersecting diagonal lines. Fold into a cone and whipstitch the two straight edges together.

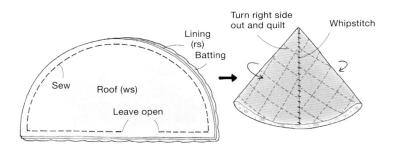

Lining (rs)
Batting
Sew
Roof (ws)
Leave open
Turn right side out and quilt
Whipstitch

2. Embroider the wings onto the bird pieces as indicated on the template. Sew the two bird pieces with right sides together, leaving an opening. Make clips in the curved seam allowances. Turn right side out. Stuff with the pellets, then hemstitch the opening closed. Complete the remaining embroidery as indicated on the template.

3. Make the tassel as shown on page 86. Tuck the tassel end into the top of the roof and sew, securing it on the inside. Sew the bird to the inside of the roof using No. 25 embroidery floss in yellow green. Blanket stitch around the bottom of the roof, then chain stitch on top of the blanket stitching as indicated on the template.

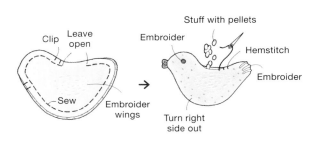

Clip
Leave open
Sew
Embroider wings
Turn right side out
Stuff with pellets
Embroider
Hemstitch
Embroider

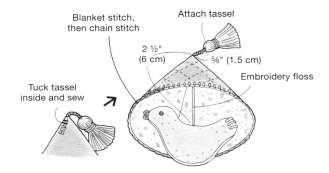

Blanket stitch, then chain stitch
Attach tassel
2 ½" (6 cm)
⅝" (1.5 cm)
Tuck tassel inside and sew
Embroidery floss

4. Align the house and lining with right sides together. Layer a piece of batting underneath. Sew, leaving an opening. Turn right side out and hemstitch the opening closed. Quilt with vertical lines about ⅜" (1 cm) apart, then quilt along the top. Appliqué the door and embroider as indicated on the templates. Make the covered buttons (refer to page 12) and hemstitch to the house.

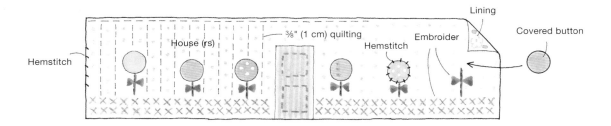

5. Align the bottom and lining with right sides together. Layer a piece of batting underneath. Sew, leaving an opening. Turn right side out and hemstitch the opening closed. Quilt with vertical lines about ⅜" (1 cm) apart. Whipstitch the two short edges of the house together, then whipstitch the bottom to the house.

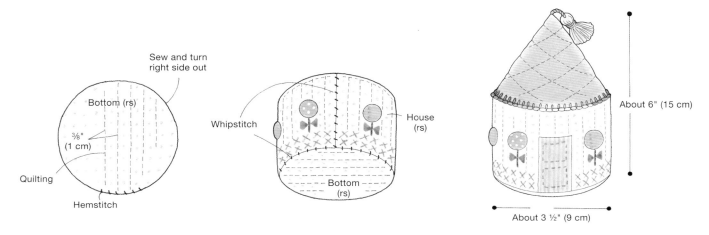

HOW TO MAKE THE TASSEL

Wrap light blue No. 5 pearl cotton around a 4" (10 cm) wide piece of cardboard 40 times. Remove the floss from the cardboard. Wrap a piece of brown No. 5 pearl cotton around the center and tie a knot, leaving 3 ⅛" (8 cm) long thread tails. Fold the tassel in half. Wrap another piece of brown floss around the tassel, about ⅜" (1 cm) from the top. Cut the loops and trim the bottom of the tassel. Blanket stitch around the thread tails using brown floss.

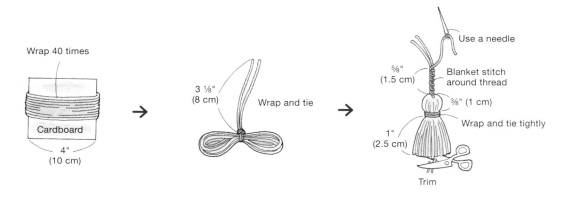

Bluebird Tea Mat

MATERIALS

- **Appliqué fabric:** Assorted scraps
- **Main fabric:** ½ yard of beige fabric
- **Backing fabric:** ½ yard of print fabric
- **Batting:** 11 ¾" x 13 ¾" (30 x 35 cm)
- Eight ½"-⅝" (1.2-1.5 cm) diameter buttons
- No. 25 embroidery floss in brown, green, and variegated purple
- Linen thread in beige
- Candlewicking floss in variegated green

CUTTING INSTRUCTIONS

Trace and cut out the templates on page 134 (refer to page 6 for instructions on using templates). Cut the following fabric pieces adding ¼" (0.7 cm) seam allowance:

- Appliqué pieces of assorted scraps
- 1 tea mat of main fabric
- 1 tea mat of backing fabric

CONSTRUCTION STEPS

Appliqué the top as indicated on the template. Align the top and backing with right sides together. Layer a piece of batting underneath. Sew around the tea mat, leaving an opening. Trim the batting seam allowances and turn right side out. Hemstitch the opening closed. Quilt with 1" (2.5 cm) squares as shown in the diagram below. Embroider and attach the buttons as indicated on the template.

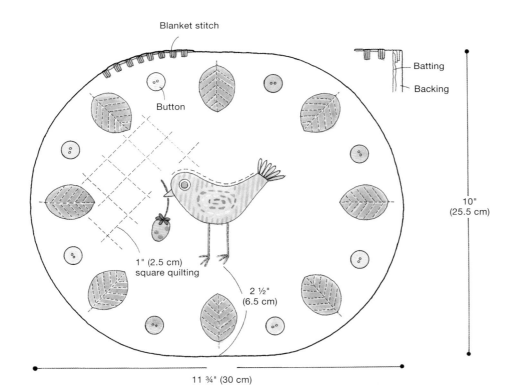

Blanket stitch

Button

Batting

Backing

1" (2.5 cm) square quilting

2 ½" (6.5 cm)

10" (25.5 cm)

11 ¾" (30 cm)

Sew using ¼" (0.7 cm) seam allowance, unless otherwise noted.

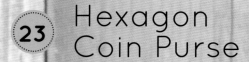

(23) Hexagon
Coin Purse

(24) Hexagon
Zip Pouch

I love little pouches and bags because they are quick to sew and they make wonderful gifts for friends. These retro hexie designs use English paper piecing, which can be quite addictive! With such a great variety of clasps and frames on the market today, you might be inspired to design your own pouches once you master the technique.

A hidden internal wire frame creates a wide opening and provides structure to the Hexagon Zip Pouch.

Pearl beads add a stylish touch to this sweet little Hexagon Coin Purse.

Hexagon Coin Purse

MATERIALS

- **Patchwork fabric:** Assorted scraps
- **Lining fabric:** ¼ yard of print fabric
- **Batting:** 6" x 13 ¾" (15 x 35 cm)
- One 2" x 4" (5 x 10 cm) sew-in metal purse clasp with pink pearl balls
- 45 3 mm diameter pearl beads
- Card stock (for English paper piecing templates)

CUTTING INSTRUCTIONS

Trace and cut out the templates on page 135 (refer to page 6 for instructions on using templates). Cut the following fabric pieces adding ¼" (0.7 cm) seam allowance:

- 66 **A** pieces of assorted scraps
- 2 purses of lining fabric

Sew using ¼" (0.7 cm) seam allowance, unless otherwise noted.

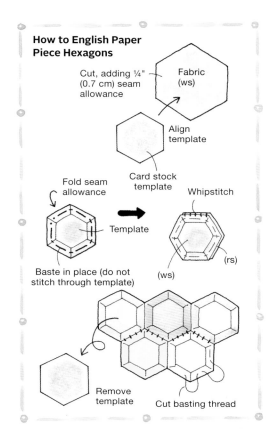

How to English Paper Piece Hexagons

Cut, adding ¼" (0.7 cm) seam allowance — Fabric (ws)

Align template

Card stock template

Fold seam allowance

Template

Whipstitch

(rs)

(ws)

Baste in place (do not stitch through template)

Remove template

Cut basting thread

CONSTRUCTION STEPS

1. Make the purse front and back using the English paper piecing technique shown in the above diagram.

2. Align the lining and front with right sides together. Layer a piece of batting underneath. Sew, leaving an opening to turn right side out. Repeat process for the purse back.

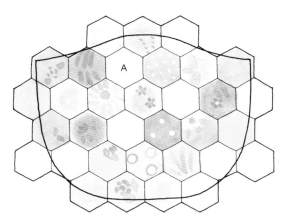

A

Sew hexagons together in general shape of purse template

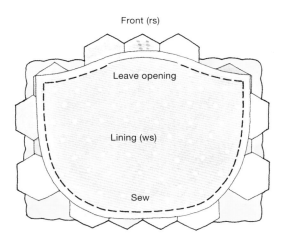

Front (rs)

Leave opening

Lining (ws)

Sew

3. Use the template on page 135 to trim the front and back into shape, making sure to leave ¼" (0.7 cm) seam allowance. Turn each piece right side out and hemstitch the opening closed. Sew the darts (refer to template for placement). Hemstitch dart seam allowances to lining. Stitch in the ditch around each hexagon. Sew the beads to each hexagon corner on the front only.

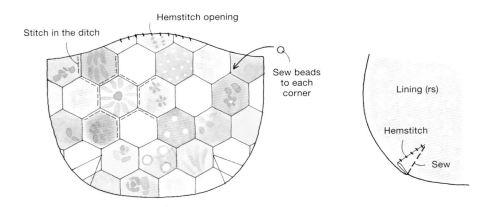

4. Align the front and back with right sides together. Whipstitch together, stitching through the top fabric only (refer to page 11). Leave the top of the purse open. Turn right side out.

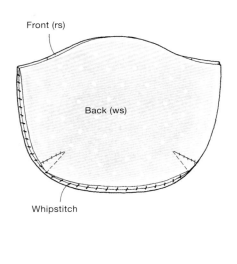

5. Align the centers and insert the purse into the opened metal clasp. Starting from the center and working toward each edge, backstitch the purse to the clasp using two strands of quilting thread.

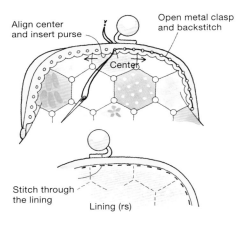

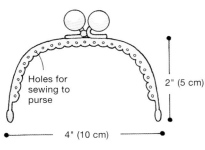

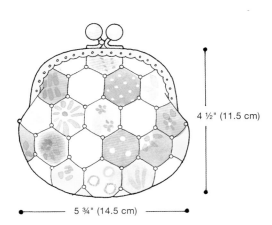

Hexagon Zip Pouch

- **Patchwork fabric:** Assorted scraps
- **Accent fabric:** ½ yard of striped fabric
- **Batting:** 9 ¾" x 13 ¾" (25 x 35 cm)
- One 10" (25.5 cm) zipper
- One set of 4" (10 cm) internal wire frames
- Four ¾" (1.8 cm) diameter covered buttons
- Card stock (for English paper piecing templates)

CUTTING INSTRUCTIONS

Trace and cut out the templates on page 135 (refer to page 6 for instructions on using templates). Cut the following fabric pieces adding ¼" (0.7 cm) seam allowance:

- 40 **A** pieces of assorted scraps
- 4 covered buttons of assorted scraps

Cut out the following pieces, which do not have templates, according to the measurements below (these measurements include seam allowance):

Accent fabric:

- Bottom: 4 ½" x 4 ½" (11.4 x 11.4 cm)
- Back: 4 ¾" x 8 ½" (12.4 x 21.4 cm)
- Bias strips (cut 2): 1 ⅛" x 9" (2.9 x 22 cm)

PATCHWORK DIAGRAM

POUCH

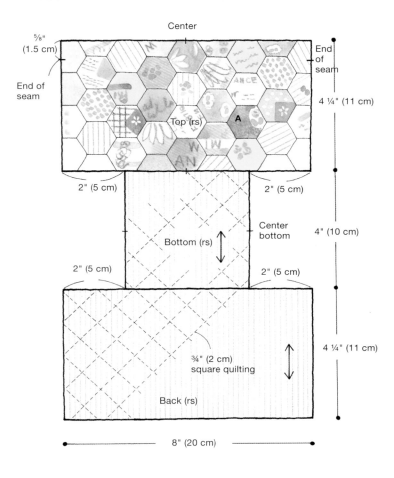

BINDING

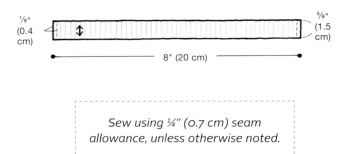

Sew using ¼" (0.7 cm) seam allowance, unless otherwise noted.

CONSTRUCTION STEPS

1. Make the pouch front using the English paper piecing technique shown in the diagram on page 89. Trim the front into a 4 ¾" x 8 ½" (12.4 x 21.4 cm) rectangle. With right sides together, sew the bottom to the front, then sew the back to the bottom. Cut the lining in the shape of the completed top. Align the lining and top with right sides together. Layer a piece of batting underneath. Sew, leaving both ends open. Turn right side out and stitch in the ditch around each hexagon. Quilt the bottom and back with ¾" (2 cm) squares.

2. Fold the bag in half with right sides together. Whip-stitch together along the sides, stitching through the top fabric only (refer to page 11). Align the side seams with the bottom fold and whipstitch to miter the corners. Fold each bias strip short edge over ¼" (0.5 cm) twice and topstitch using ⅛" (0.4 cm) seam allowance. With right sides together, sew bias strips to pouch top along opening. Fold the bias strips to the inside of the pouch and hemstitch to the lining. This will be the casing for the internal wire frame.

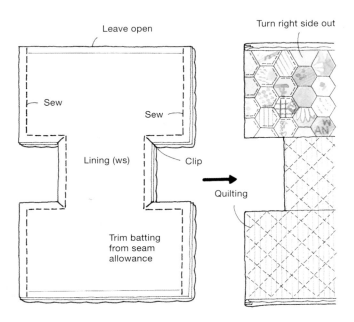

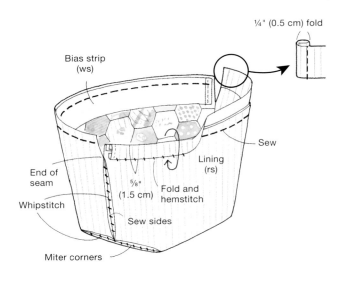

3. Hemstitch the zipper to the pouch opening. Sew the two sides of the zipper together at the end. Make the covered buttons and attach to the zipper ends (refer to page 12). Insert each section of the internal wire frame through the casing.

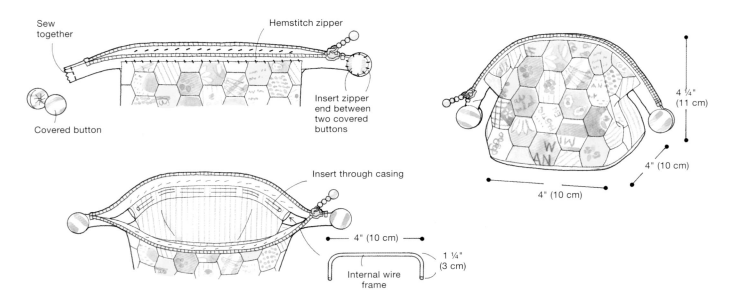

25 Tea Time Pouch

26 Owl Coin Purse

I always carry a handmade pouch inside my bag, just like a good luck charm! Embellished with the traditional Sunbonnet Sue quilting motif, this teacup-shaped pouch makes a great gift for quilter friends. As a Japanese symbol of happiness, this quirky owl-shaped pouch always offers a friendly face.

Tea Time Pouch

MATERIALS

- **Patchwork and appliqué fabric:** Assorted scraps
- **Main fabric:** ¼ yard of pink fabric

- **Accent fabric:** ⅛ yard of beige fabric
- **Lining fabric:** ¼ yard of print fabric
- **Batting:** 9 ¾" x 15 ¾" (25 x 40 cm)

- One 7" (18 cm) zipper
- No. 25 embroidery floss in red, green, light blue, and variegated brown

CUTTING INSTRUCTIONS

Trace and cut out the templates on page 136 (refer to page 6 for instructions on using templates). Cut the following fabric pieces adding ¼" (0.7 cm) seam allowance:

- Patchwork pieces of assorted scraps
- Appliqué pieces of assorted scraps
- 2 teacups of lining fabric
- 1 bottom of main fabric
- 1 bottom of lining fabric

- 1 zipper charm of assorted scraps (cut without seam allowance)

Cut out the following pieces, which do not have templates, according to the measurements below (these measurements include seam allowance):

Main fabric:
- Handle (cut on the bias): 1 ½" x 7" (4 x 18 cm)
- Bias strips: ½ yard (0.5 m) of 1 ½" (3.5 cm) wide bias strips

CONSTRUCTION STEPS

Sew using ¼" (0.7 cm) seam allowance, unless otherwise noted.

1. Sew the patchwork pieces together to make the front. Appliqué and embroider as indicated on the template. Align the top and lining with right sides together. Layer a piece of batting underneath. Sew around three sides, leaving the top of the teacup open. Repeat process to make the back.

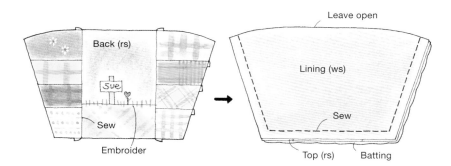

2. Trim the batting seam allowances and turn right side out. Quilt as indicated on the template. Embellish with the feather stitch as indicated on the template.

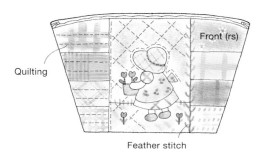

3. Align the bottom and lining with right sides together. Layer a piece of batting underneath. Sew, leaving an opening. Trim the batting seam allowances and turn right side out. Hemstitch the opening closed. Quilt as indicated on the template.

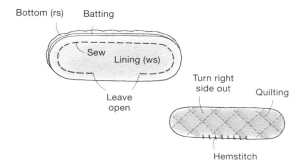

4. To make the handle, roll a 6"
(15 cm) long scrap of batting into a
cylinder and hemstitch in place. Fold
and press one of the long edges of
the handle fabric over ¼" (0.5 cm).
Wrap the fabric around the cylinder of
batting so the long edges of the fabric
overlap ¼" (0.5 cm) and hemstitch.
Fold and press each short edge over
¼" (0.5 cm). Running stitch around the
short ends as close to the fold as possible, leaving long thread tails. Pull the
thread tails to gather the fabric around
the batting and knot to secure.

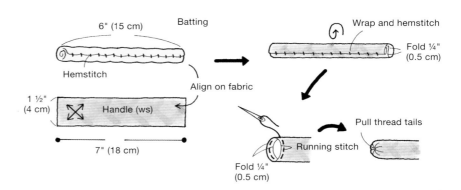

6" (15 cm)   Batting
Hemstitch

1 ½"
(4 cm)   Handle (ws)   Align on fabric
7" (18 cm)

Wrap and hemstitch
Fold ¼"
(0.5 cm)

Running stitch

Fold ¼"
(0.5 cm)

Pull thread tails

5. Align the front and back with right
sides together. Sandwich the handle in
between the front and back (refer to
the template for placement). Whipstitch the front and back together
along the sides, stitching through the
top fabric only (refer to page 11). With
right sides together, whipstitch the
bottom to the pouch, stitching through
the top fabric only once again.

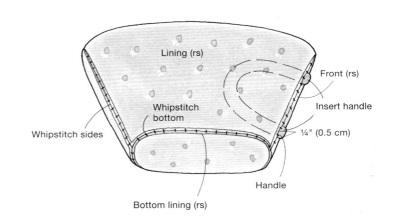

Lining (rs)

Front (rs)

Insert handle

Whipstitch
bottom

¼" (0.5 cm)

Whipstitch sides

Handle

Bottom lining (rs)

6. Use the bias strips to bind the pouch opening. Sew the zipper to the binding as shown below. Make the zipper charm
(refer to page 12).

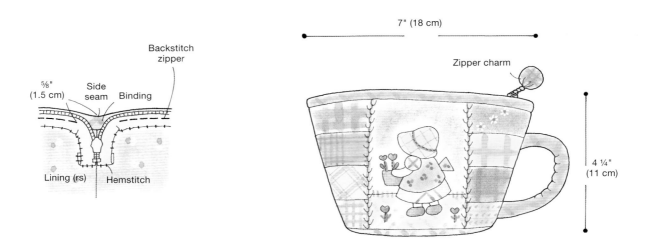

Backstitch
zipper

⅝"
(1.5 cm)   Side
seam   Binding

Lining (rs)   Hemstitch

7" (18 cm)

Zipper charm

4 ¼"
(11 cm)

Owl Coin Purse

MATERIALS

- **Main fabric:** ¼ yard of dark brown fabric
- **Accent fabric:** ⅛ yard of gray fabric
- **Lining fabric:** ¼ yard of print fabric
- **Batting:** 6" x 13 ¾" (15 x 35 cm)
- **Felt:**
  - Brown: 1 ½" x 2 ¾" (4 x 7 cm)
  - White: 1 ¼" x 2" (3 x 5 cm)
  - Navy: ¾" x 1 ½" (2 x 4 cm)
  - Light yellow: ¾" x ¾" (2 x 2 cm)
- 4 ¾" (12 cm) of 1 mm diameter waxed cotton cord
- Two ⅝" (1.5 cm) diameter cover buttons
- 1 ¼" x 2 ½" (3 x 6 cm) scrap of fabric
- One 4" (10 cm) zipper
- No. 25 embroidery floss in brown, green, light blue, and light yellow
- No. 5 pearl cotton in dark brown

CUTTING INSTRUCTIONS

Trace and cut out the templates on page 137 (refer to page 6 for instructions on using templates). Cut the following fabric pieces adding ¼" (0.7 cm) seam allowance:

- 1 front of main fabric
- 1 front of lining fabric
- 1 upper back of main fabric
- 1 upper back of lining fabric
- 1 lower back of main fabric
- 4 wings of accent fabric*

*The wings should be symmetrical. Use the right side of the template for one set and the wrong side of the template for the other.

Cut out the following fabric pieces without adding seam allowance:

- Appliqué pieces of felt
- 2 zipper charms of scrap fabric

Sew using ¼" (0.7 cm) seam allowance, unless otherwise noted.

CONSTRUCTION STEPS

1. Align the front and lining with right sides together. Layer a piece of batting underneath. Sew, leaving an opening. Make clips in the inner curves and trim the batting seam allowances. Turn right side out. Hemstitch the opening closed. Appliqué the felt pieces to the front as indicated on the template. Use the embroidery floss to quilt as indicated on the template.

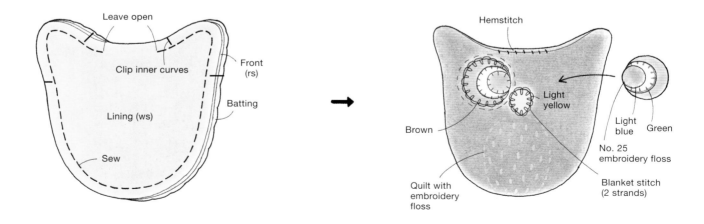

2. Align the upper back and lining with right sides together. Layer a piece of batting underneath. Sew, leaving an opening (as indicated by the ☆ on the template) . Trim the batting seam allowances and turn right side out. Hemstitch the opening closed. Quilt with vertical lines. Follow the same process to make the lower back. Backstitch and hemstitch one side of the zipper to the upper back lining and the other side to the lower back lining. Fold the short ends of the zipper over ¼" (0.5 cm) twice and hemstitch to the zipper tape. Hemstitch the zipper to the upper and lower backs on the pouch outside. Make sure the zipper is open. With right sides together, whipstitch the front and back together around all edges, stitching through the top fabric only (refer to page 11). Turn right side out through the open zipper.

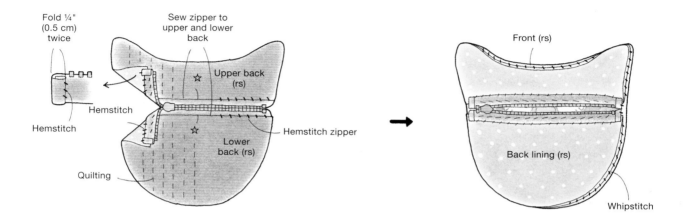

3. Align two matching wing pieces with right sides together. Layer a piece of batting underneath. Sew, leaving an opening. Trim the batting seam allowances and turn right side out. Hemstitch the opening closed. Blanket stitch around the wing using dark brown No. 5 pearl cotton. Follow the same process to make another symmetrical wing. Hemstitch the wings to the pouch following the placement indicated on the template.

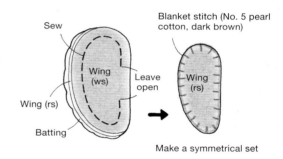

Make a symmetrical set

4. Make the covered buttons (refer to page 12). Thread the cord through the zipper pull. Sew the covered buttons around the cord ends.

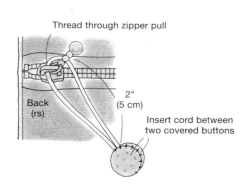

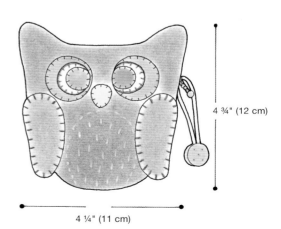

Appliquéd Sewing Box

To us quilters, our sewing boxes rank among our prized possessions. In fact, my sewing box is one of the items I'd choose to bring with me if I were to be stranded on a desert island. This design is dedicated to those who love sewing as much as I do.

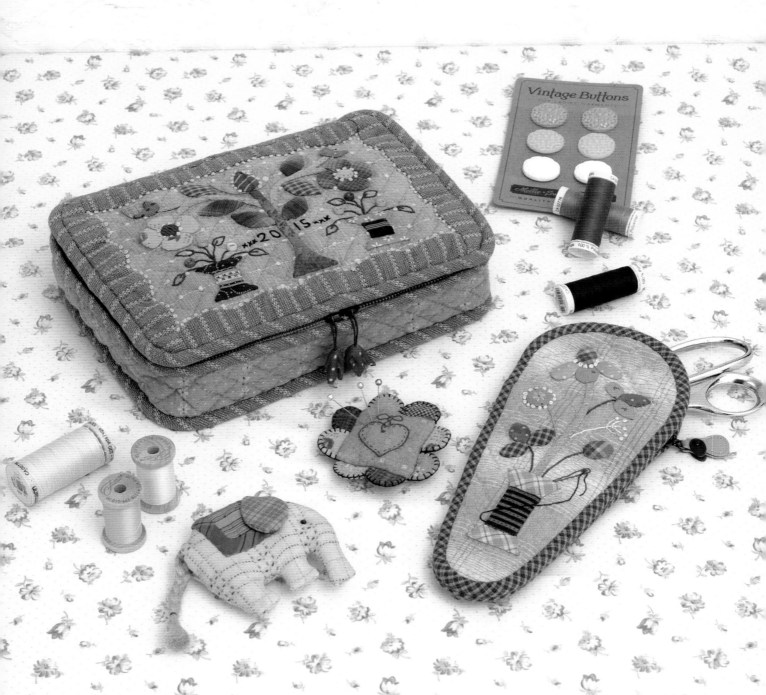

The interior of the sewing box features dividers and pockets perfect for storing thread, needles, and other notions. This special case is convenient for transporting your tools to quilting classes.

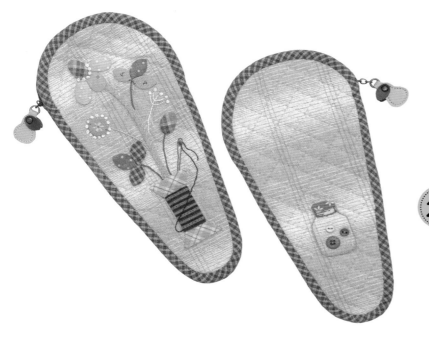

28 # Floral Scissor Caddy

Sealed with a zipper, this ingenious little case keeps your scissors safe and secure. The inside is divided into two compartments, allowing you to store two pairs of scissors at once.

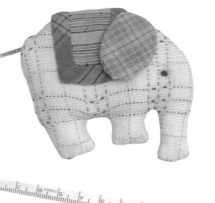

29 # Elephant Tape Measure Case

This cute little elephant makes me smile everytime I reach for my tape measure! Just pull the braided tail to reveal the tape measure.

30 # Flower Pin Cushion

This sweet pin cushion is a perfect use for your favorite scraps. Embellish with embroidery for a special touch.

Appliquéd Sewing Box

MATERIALS

- **Appliqué fabric:** Assorted scraps
- **Main fabric:** ½ yard of brown striped fabric
- **Accent fabric #1:** ¼ yard of pink fabric
- **Accent fabric #2:** ¼ yard of blue fabric
- **Zipper charm/yoyo fabric:** ⅛ yard of red fabric
- **Lining fabric:** 1 yard of print fabric

- **Batting:** 11 ¾" x 43 ¼" (30 x 110 cm)
- **Lightweight fusible interfacing:** 6" x 19 ¾" (15 x 50 cm)
- Two 11" (28 cm) zippers
- One 9" (23 cm) zipper
- Six ¼" (0.6 cm) diameter buttons
- 23 ¾" (60 cm) of ⅜" (1 cm) wide lace

- 6" (15 cm) of 1 mm diameter waxed cotton cord
- No. 25 embroidery floss in brown and dark brown
- Candlewicking floss in off-white

PATCHWORK DIAGRAM

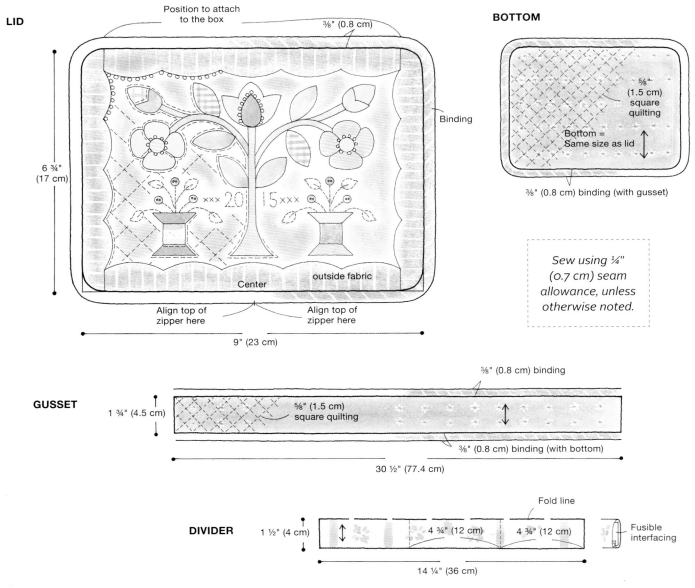

LID

Position to attach to the box

⅜" (0.8 cm)

Binding

6 ¾" (17 cm)

×××20   15×××

outside fabric

Center

Align top of zipper here

Align top of zipper here

9" (23 cm)

BOTTOM

⅝" (1.5 cm) square quilting

Bottom = Same size as lid

⅜" (0.8 cm) binding (with gusset)

Sew using ¼" (0.7 cm) seam allowance, unless otherwise noted.

GUSSET

1 ¾" (4.5 cm)

⅜" (0.8 cm) binding

⅝" (1.5 cm) square quilting

⅜" (0.8 cm) binding (with bottom)

30 ½" (77.4 cm)

DIVIDER

1 ½" (4 cm)

Fold line

4 ¾" (12 cm)   4 ¾" (12 cm)

Fusible interfacing

14 ¼" (36 cm)

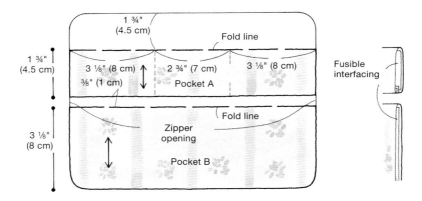

CUTTING INSTRUCTIONS

Trace and cut out the templates on page 138 (refer to page 6 for instructions on using templates). Cut the following fabric pieces adding ¼" (0.7 cm) seam allowance:

- Appliqué pieces of assorted scraps
- Appliqué borders of main fabric
- 1 lid of accent fabric #1
- 1 lid of lining fabric
- 1 bottom of accent fabric #2
- 1 bottom of lining fabric
- 2 yoyos of zipper charm/yoyo fabric (do not add seam allowance)

Cut out the following pieces, which do not have templates, according to the measurements below (these measurements include seam allowance):

Lining fabric:
- Pocket A: 4" x 9 ½" (10.4 x 24.4 cm)

- Pocket B: 6 ¾" x 9 ½" (17.4 x 24.4 cm)
- Gusset lining: 2 ¼" x 32" (5.9 x 81.4 cm)
- Divider: 3 ½" x 14 ¾" (9.4 x 37.4 cm)

Fusible interfacing:
- Pocket A: 1 ¾" x 9" (4.5 x 23 cm)
- Pocket B: 3 ⅛" x 9" (8 x 23 cm)
- Divider: 1 ½" x 14 ¼" (4 x 36 cm)

Accent fabric #2:
- Gusset: 2 ¼" x 31" (5.9 x 78.8 cm)

Main fabric:
- Bias strips: 2 ¾ yards (2.75 m) of 1 ½" (3.5 cm) wide bias strips

Zipper charm/yoyo fabric:
- Zipper charms (cut 2): 2 ½" x 2 ½" (6 x 6 cm)

CONSTRUCTION STEPS

1. Appliqué and embroider the lid as indicated on the template. Layer the lid, batting, and lining. Quilt as indicated on the template. Embroider with colonial knots as indicated on the template, stitching through the lining.

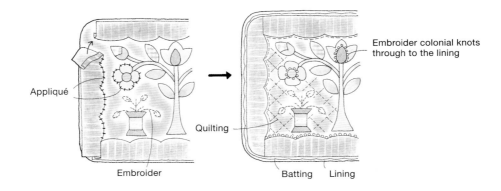

2. Fold pocket A in half with right sides together. Adhere fusible interfacing to the wrong side of one half. Sew the long edges together, then turn right side out. Adhere fusible interfacing to the wrong side of one half of pocket B. Fold pocket B in half with right sides facing out. Sew pockets A and B to the wrong side of the 9" (23 cm) zipper, stitching as close to the zipper as possible as shown at right.

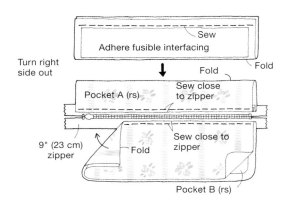

3. Align the pocket on top of the lid lining. Baste around three sides. Backstitch to divide pocket A into three sections, making sure not to stitch through to the top of the lid. The sections should be 3 ⅛" (8 cm), 2 ¾" (7 cm), and 3 ⅛" (8 cm) wide.

4. Fold the divider in half with right sides together. Adhere fusible interfacing to the wrong side of one half. Sew around three sides, leaving an opening. Turn right side out and hemstitch the opening closed. Mark the divider to create three 4 ¾" (12 cm) wide sections.

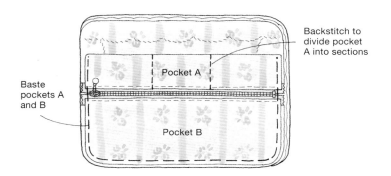

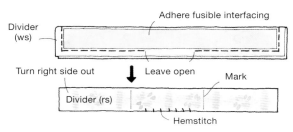

5. Layer the gusset, batting, and lining. Quilt with ⅝" (1.5 cm) squares. Fold the gusset in half with right sides together. Use the technique shown on page 11 to sew the short ends together and finish the seam allowance using the lining.

6. Layer the bottom, batting, and lining. Quilt with ⅝" (1.5 cm) squares. Sew the right side of the gusset to the bottom lining. Use the bias strips to bind the seam allowance and to bind the top of the gusset. Backstitch the divider to the gusset lining following the marks made in step 4. Make sure not to stitch through to the right side of the gusset.

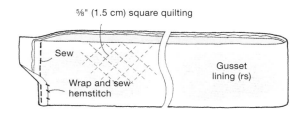

7. Position one of the zipper charm pieces with the wrong side facing up. Fold the four corners in so they meet in the middle and press. Fold the four points in so they meet in the middle again. Make a hole in the center of the square. Cut the cord in half and insert one piece through the zipper pull. Insert the cord ends through the hole in the fabric and knot. Running stitch the fabric as shown below, leaving long thread tails. Pull the tread tails to gather the fabric into a flower shape. Repeat for the other zipper charm. Use pliers to remove the zipper pull.

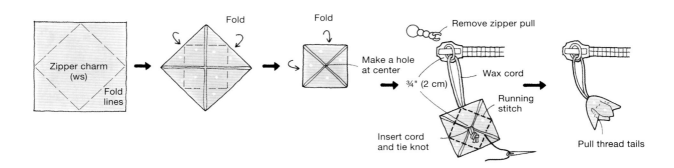

8. Use the bias strips to bind the lid. Sew the two 11" (28 cm) zippers to the sewing box as shown below. Sew the lace to the zipper tape on the inside of the lid only. To make the yoyo, fold the seam allowance over ⅛" (0.3 cm). Running stitch in the seam allowance as close to the fold as possible, leaving long thread tails. Pull the thread tails taut and knot to complete the yoyo. Hemstitch the yoyo to the inside of the sewing box to cover the zipper ends. Repeat to make and attach another yoyo. Sew the buttons to the top of the lid.

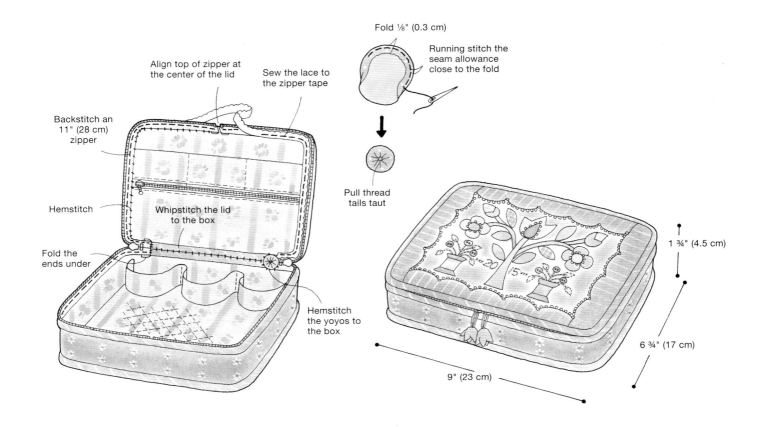

Floral Scissor Caddy

MATERIALS

- **Appliqué fabric:** Assorted scraps
- **Main fabric:** ⅓ yard of pink fabric
- **Lining fabric:** ⅓ yard of print fabric
- **Pocket fabric:** ⅓ yard of pink fabric
- **Binding fabric:** Two 1 ½" x 23 ¾" (3.5 x 60 cm) bias strips

- **Batting:** 9 ¾" x 9 ¾" (25 x 25 cm)
- **Lightweight fusible interfacing:** 6 ¾" x 9 ¾" (17 x 25 cm)
- One 7" (18 cm) zipper
- Two ¼" (0.6 cm) diameter buttons
- One ⅜" (1 cm) diameter button

- One zipper charm
- No. 25 embroidery floss in light green, off-white, dark brown, green, light brown, light blue, and red

CUTTING INSTRUCTIONS

Trace and cut out the templates on page 139 (refer to page 6 for instructions on using templates). Cut the following fabric pieces adding ¼" (0.7 cm) seam allowance:

- 1 front of main fabric
- 1 back of main fabric
- 1 front of lining fabric
- 1 back of lining fabric
- 2 pockets of pocket fabric (cut on the fold)
- 2 pockets of fusible interfacing

Cut out the following pieces, which do not have templates, according to the measurement below (this measurement includes seam allowance):

Binding fabric:

- Bias strips: Two 1 ½" x 23 ¾" (3.5 x 60 cm) bias strips

Sew using ¼" (0.7 cm) seam allowance, unless otherwise noted.

CONSTRUCTION STEPS

1. Appliqué and embroider the front and back as indicated on the templates. Sew the buttons to the back. Layer the front, batting and lining. Quilt with squares as indicated on the template. Follow the same process to quilt the back.

2. Adhere fusible interfacing to the wrong side of one half of the pocket. Fold the pocket in half with right sides facing out. Running stitch ⅛" (0.3 cm) away from the fold using two strands of dark brown floss. Repeat for the other pocket.

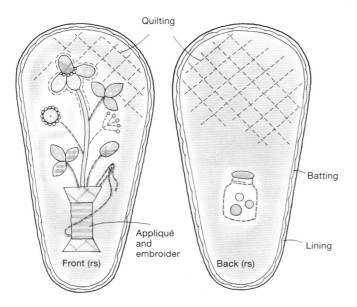

Quilting

Front (rs)

Appliqué and embroider

Back (rs)

Batting

Lining

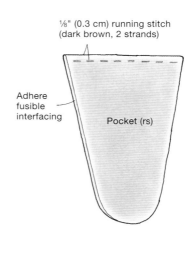

⅛" (0.3 cm) running stitch (dark brown, 2 strands)

Adhere fusible interfacing

Pocket (rs)

3. Align the pockets on top of the linings and baste. Use the bias strips to bind the front and back. Align the right side of the zipper with the binding on the linings following the placement indicated on the template. Sew one half of the zipper to the front lining and the other half to the back lining as shown below.

4. Make sure the zipper is open. Align the front and back with right sides together. Whipstitch together starting and stopping at the ends of the zipper.

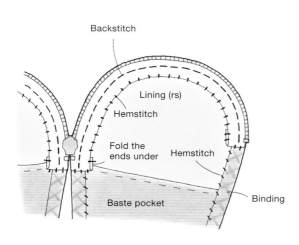

Backstitch

Lining (rs)

Hemstitch

Fold the ends under

Hemstitch

Baste pocket

Binding

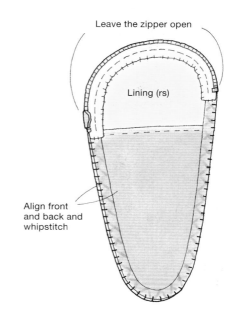

Leave the zipper open

Lining (rs)

Align front and back and whipstitch

5. Turn right side out through the open zipper. Use pliers to remove the zipper pull and attach the zipper charm.

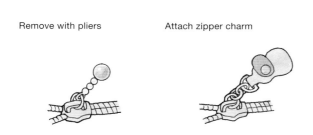

Remove with pliers

Attach zipper charm

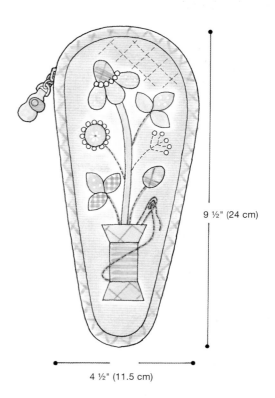

9 ½" (24 cm)

4 ½" (11.5 cm)

Elephant Tape Measure Case

MATERIALS

- **Main fabric:** ¼ yard of yellow fabric
- **Ear fabric:** ¼ yard of pink fabric
- **Blanket fabric:** ⅛ yard of striped fabric
- **Binding fabric:** 1" x 11 ¾" (2.5 x 30 cm) bias strip
- **Lining fabric:** ¼ yard of white fabric
- **Batting:** 6" x 9 ¾" (15 x 25 cm)
- Two round brown beads
- 29 ½" (75 cm) of linen string
- Scrap of embroidery floss
- Polyester stuffing
- 2" (5 cm) diameter tape measure

CUTTING INSTRUCTIONS

Trace and cut out the templates on page 140 (refer to page 6 for instructions on using templates). Cut the following fabric pieces adding ¼" (0.7 cm) seam allowance:

- 1 blanket of blanket fabric (cut on the fold)
- 4 ears of ear fabric (cut on the bias)

Cut out the following piece, which does not have a template, according to the measurement below (this measurement includes seam allowance):

Binding fabric:

- Bias strip: 1" x 11 ¾" (2.5 x 30 cm) bias strip

CONSTRUCTION STEPS

Sew using ¼" (0.7 cm) seam allowance, unless otherwise noted.

1. Trace the elephant template onto the wrong side of a piece of lining fabric. Align the lining and main fabric with right sides together. Layer a piece of batting underneath. Sew along the traced line, leaving an opening. Cut the elephant out, leaving ¼" (0.5 cm) seam allowance. Make clips in the curved sections of the seam allowance. Trim the batting seam allowance and turn right side out. Hemstitch the opening closed. Repeat the process using the wrong side of the template to make another symmetrical elephant. Use the bias strip to bind the blanket. Align two ear pieces with right sides together. Sew, leaving an opening. Turn right side out and hemstitch the opening closed. Repeat to make the other ear.

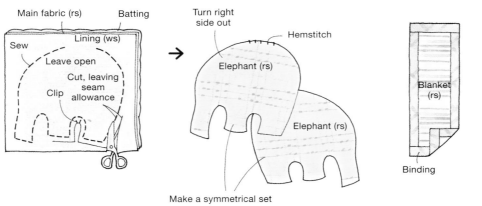

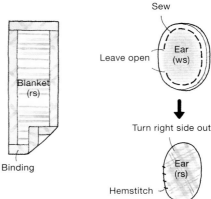

2. Align the two elephant halves with right sides facing out. Sandwich the tape measure in between so the end of the tape is positioned at the rear of the elephant. Whipstitch the elephant halves together, inserting bits of stuffing into the legs and nose as you sew. Make sure to leave the top of the elephant open.

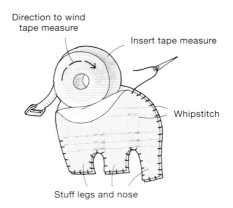

3. Insert stuffing around the tape measure. Whipstitch the top of the elephant closed, leaving a small opening for the end of the tape as indicated on the template. Align the point a's and hemstitch the ears to the head. Hemstitch the blanket to the elephant's back. Sew the beads to the head following the placement indicated on the template. Insert three 9 ¾" (25 cm) long pieces of linen string through the slit at the end of the tape. Fold the string in half so there are six strands. Separate the strands into groups of two and braid to create a 2 ¾" (7 cm) long tail. Wrap a scrap of embroidery floss around the end of the braid and tie a knot. Cut the linen string ¾" (2 cm) below the knot.

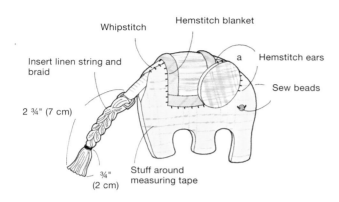

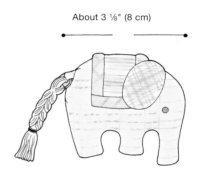

About 3 ⅛" (8 cm)

Flower Pin Cushion

MATERIALS

- **Petal fabric:** Assorted scraps
- **Main fabric:** 2 ¾" x 6" (7 x 15 cm) of pink fabric
- **Polyester stuffing**
- No. 25 embroidery floss in brown and dark brown

CUTTING INSTRUCTIONS

Trace and cut out the templates on page 140 (refer to page 6 for instructions on using templates). Cut the following fabric pieces adding ¼" (0.7 cm) seam allowance:

- 16 petals of eight different assorted scraps
- 2 pin cushions of main fabric

CONSTRUCTION STEPS

1. Align two matching petals with right sides together. Sew around the curve, leaving the bottom open. Trim the seam allowance to ⅛" (0.3 cm) and turn right side out. Blanket stitch around the curve using two strands of dark brown embroidery floss. Repeat the process to make seven more petals.

2. Embroider one of the pin cushion pieces as indicated on the template. With right sides together, align two petals at the center of each edge of the embroidered pin cushion piece. Baste the petals in place. With the right side facing down, align the other pin cushion piece on top and sew around three sides. Turn right side out. Stuff the pin cushion, then hemstitch the opening closed.

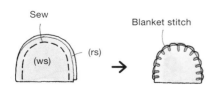

Sew using ¼" (0.7 cm) seam allowance, unless otherwise noted.

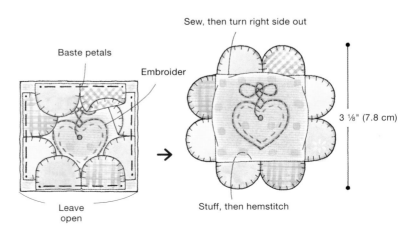

31 Floral Basket

32 Floral Coasters

Time to bust out your scrap stash! These hexie projects are a wonderful way to showcase your favorite fabrics. Combine several flower motifs to create a basket, or use the motifs individually as coasters.

Slip the patchwork over a store-bought wire basket to create a custom piece.

Floral Basket

MATERIALS

- **Patchwork fabric:** Assorted scraps
- **Main fabric:** ¼ yard of beige fabric
- **Lining fabric:** ¼ yard of print fabric
- **Batting:** 8" x 43 ¼" (20 x 110 cm)
- One 13" (32 cm) handle

CUTTING INSTRUCTIONS

Trace and cut out the templates on page 141 (refer to page 6 for instructions on using templates). Cut the following fabric pieces adding ¼" (0.7 cm) seam allowance:

- 40 **A** pieces of assorted scraps
- 16 **B** pieces of assorted scraps
- 8 **C** pieces of assorted scraps
- 8 stems of assorted scraps

- 1 bottom of main fabric
- 1 bottom of lining fabric

Cut out the following piece, which does not have a template, according to the measurement below (this measurement includes seam allowance):

Main fabric:
- Background fabric: 2 ½" x 29 ¼" (6.5 x 74.4 cm)

Sew using ¼" (0.7 cm) seam allowance, unless otherwise noted.

PATCHWORK DIAGRAM

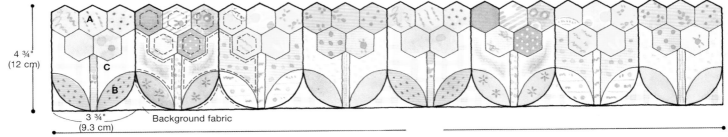

4 ¾" (12 cm)

3 ¾" (9.3 cm)

Background fabric

29 ¼" (74.4 cm)

CONSTRUCTION STEPS

1. Use the A pieces to make eight flowers using the English paper piecing technique shown in the diagram on page 89. Hemstitch the flowers, stems, and B and C pieces together. Sew the eight flowers together. Hemstitch the assembled flowers to the background fabric.

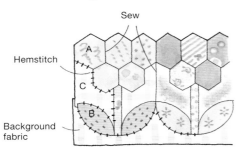

Sew

Hemstitch

A

C

B

Background fabric

2. Cut the lining in the shape of the assembled top. Align the lining and top with right sides together. Layer a piece of batting underneath. Sew, leaving an opening. Make clips into the seam allowance at the hexagon corners.

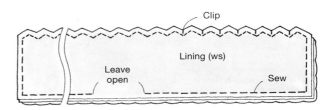

Clip

Leave open

Lining (ws)

Sew

3. Trim the batting seam allowance and turn right side out. Hemstitch the opening closed. Quilt as indicated on the template. Align the bottom and lining with right sides together. Layer a piece of batting underneath. Sew, leaving an opening. Trim the batting seam allowance and turn right side out. Hemstitch the opening closed. Quilt with ¾" (2 cm) squares.

4. Whipstitch the short ends of the basket together, stitching through the top fabric only (refer to page 11), then whipstitch the bottom to the basket. Backstitch the handle to the basket using two strands of quilting thread.

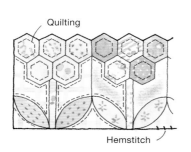

Quilting

Hemstitch

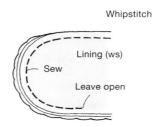

Lining (ws)

Sew

Leave open

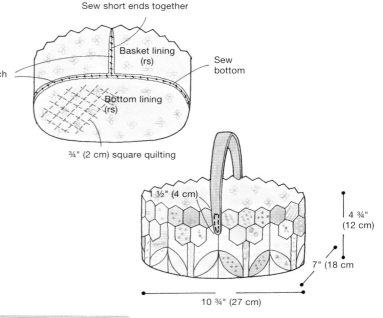

Sew short ends together

Whipstitch

Basket lining (rs)

Sew bottom

Bottom lining (rs)

¾" (2 cm) square quilting

1 ½" (4 cm)

4 ¾" (12 cm)

7" (18 cm)

10 ¾" (27 cm)

Floral Coasters

MATERIALS (for one coaster)

- **Patchwork fabric:** Assorted scraps
- **Backing fabric:** ¼ yard of print fabric
- **Batting:** 4 ¾" x 6" (12 x 15 cm)

CUTTING INSTRUCTIONS

Trace and cut out the templates on page 141 (refer to page 6 for instructions on using templates).

Cut the following fabric pieces adding ¼" (0.7 cm) seam allowance:

- 5 **A** pieces of assorted scraps
- 2 **B** pieces of assorted scraps
- 1 **C** piece of assorted scraps
- 1 stem of assorted scraps
- 1 coaster of lining fabric

Sew using ¼" (0.7 cm) seam allowance, unless otherwise noted.

CONSTRUCTION STEPS

Use the A pieces to make a flower using the English paper piecing technique shown in the diagram on page 89. Hemstitch the flower to the stem and pieces B and C. Align the assembled top and lining with right sides together. Layer a piece of batting underneath. Sew, leaving an opening. Make clips into the seam allowance at the hexagon corners and trim the excess seam allowance. Turn right side out and hemstitch the opening closed. Quilt as indicated on the template.

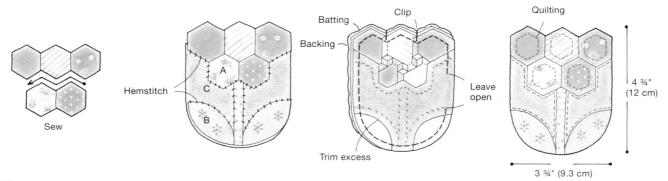

Sew

Hemstitch

A

C

B

Batting

Backing

Clip

Leave open

Trim excess

Quilting

4 ¾" (12 cm)

3 ¾" (9.3 cm)

33 Pastoral Wall Hanging

34 Countryside Collage

These sweet little appliqué projects are another great use for your scraps. With idyllic scenes from country life, these handstitched designs will add warmth and coziness to your own home.

Pastoral Wall Hanging

- **Background and appliqué fabric:** Assorted scraps
- **Backing fabric:** ¼ yard of white fabric
- **Batting:** 6" x 13 ¾" (15 x 35 cm)
- No. 25 embroidery floss in yellow, brown, white, and green
- Lightweight yarn in brown, yellow, and green
- Frame with a 4" x 11 ¾" (10 x 30 cm) window

CUTTING INSTRUCTIONS

Trace and cut out the templates on page 142 (refer to page 6 for instructions on using templates). Cut the following fabric pieces adding ¼" (0.7 cm) seam allowance:

- Background and appliqué pieces of assorted scraps (do not add seam allowance when cutting the sheep pieces)

Cut out the following piece, which does not have a template, according to the measurement below (this measurement includes seam allowance):

Backing fabric:
- Backing: 6" x 13 ¾" (15 x 35 cm)

CONSTRUCTION STEPS

1. Appliqué the pieces to the background fabric following the placement indicated on the template (refer to page 7 for appliqué instructions).

2. Layer the appliquéd fabric, batting, and backing. Embroider as indicated on the templates.

3. Wrap the fabric around the frame backing and insert into the frame.

Countryside Collage

MATERIALS

- **Background and appliqué fabric:** Assorted scraps
- **Backing fabric:** ¼ yard of white fabric
- **Batting:** 8" x 8" (20 x 20 cm)
- No. 25 embroidery floss in brown, green, orange, beige, pink, blue, light pink, yellow, light blue, light yellow, ocher, off-white, dark pink, and variegated multicolor)
- Frame with four 3" (7.5 cm) square windows

CUTTING INSTRUCTIONS

Trace and cut out the templates on page 143 (refer to page 6 for instructions on using templates). Cut the following fabric pieces adding ¼" (0.7 cm) seam allowance:

- Background and appliqué pieces of assorted scraps

Cut out the following piece, which does not have a template, according to the measurement below (this measurement includes seam allowance):

Backing fabric:
- Backing: 8" x 8" (20 x 20 cm)

CONSTRUCTION STEPS

1. Appliqué the pieces to the background fabric following the placement indicated on the template to create the four blocks (refer to page 7 for appliqué instructions).

2. Mark the position of the frame windows on the batting. Baste the four blocks to the batting following these marks. Layer the backing underneath the batting. Embroider as indicated on page 113.

3. Wrap the fabric around the frame backing and insert into the frame.

STITCH GUIDE (SEE PAGE 143 FOR FULL-SIZE TEMPLATES)

Sheep faces: Satin stitch (brown, 1 strand)
Sheep ears: Lazy daisy stitch (brown, 1 strand)
Sheep feet: Straight stitch (brown, 1 strand)
Tree trunks: Outline stitch (brown, 2 strands)
Tree branches: Straight stitch (green, 1 strand)
Flowers: French knots (orange and beige, 1 strand)
Leaves: Straight stitch (green, 1 strand)

Hat: Blanket stitch (pink, 1 strand)
Bag: Blanket stitch (blue, 1 strand)
Roof: Blanket stitch (blue, 2 strands),
Footpath: Blanket stitch (brown, 2 strands)
Bag handle: Outline stitch (blue, 1 strand)
Tree trunks: Outline stitch (brown, 2 strands)
Flowers: French knots (orange and light pink, 1 strand)
Leaves: Straight stitch (green, 1 strand)

Straight stitch (light blue, 2 strands)

Straight stitch (orange, 2 strands)

Straight stitch (off-white, 2 strands)

Satin stitch (brown, 1 strand)

Straight stitch (brown, 1 strand)

Leaf veins: Outline stitch (green, 1 strand)
Branch: Outline stitch (green, 2 strands)
Eye: French knot (brown, 2 strands)
Beak: Straight stitch (yellow, 2 strands)
Feet: Outline stitch (brown, 2 strands)
Tail: Blanket stitch (orange, 2 strands)
Wing: Running stitch (variegated multicolor, 1 strand)

Bird outline: Blanket stitch (light yellow, 2 strands)
Eye: French knot (brown, 2 strands)
Beak: Straight stitch (ocher, 2 strands)
Feet: Satin stitch (ocher, 2 strands)
Fence: Straight stitch (off-white, 2 strands)

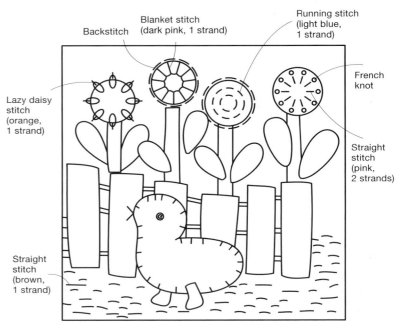

Backstitch

Blanket stitch (dark pink, 1 strand)

Running stitch (light blue, 1 strand)

Lazy daisy stitch (orange, 1 strand)

French knot

Straight stitch (pink, 2 strands)

Straight stitch (brown, 1 strand)

Quilt As You Go Sampler

I often fantasize about making large quilts, but very rarely have the time to start such a big undertaking. So instead, I enjoy making mini quilts, then connecting them to form a larger work. I've included twelve of my favorite block designs with this sampler quilt.

These blocks also make great mats or mug rugs!

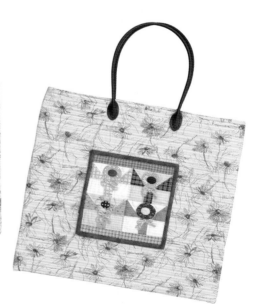

36 Quilt Block Totes

These block designs can also be used for smaller projects, such as tote bags. I like to make a simple tote bag, then attach a quilted block to form a pocket.

Quilt As You Go Sampler

MATERIALS (for one block)

- **Patchwork and appliqué fabric:** Assorted scraps
- **Backing fabric:** ¼ yard of print fabric
- **Binding fabric:** ¼ yard of print fabric
- **Batting:** 8" x 8" (20 x 20 cm)
- No. 25 embroidery floss, lace, and buttons (as needed)

CUTTING INSTRUCTIONS

Trace and cut out the block templates on Pattern Sheet A (refer to page 6 for instructions on using templates). Cut the following fabric pieces adding ¼" (0.7 cm) seam allowance:

- Patchwork pieces of assorted scraps
- Appliqué pieces of assorted scraps

Cut out the following pieces, which do not have templates, according to the measurements on the right (these measurements include seam allowance):

Backing fabric:
- Backing: 7 ¼" x 7 ¼" (18.4 x 18.4 cm)
- Binding strips (cut lengthwise): 31 ½" (80 cm) of 1 ½" (3.5 cm) wide strips

Sew using ¼" (0.7 cm) seam allowance, unless otherwise noted.

PATCHWORK DIAGRAM

BLOCK

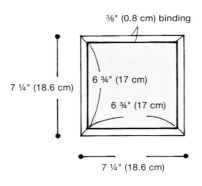

⅜" (0.8 cm) binding
6 ¾" (17 cm)
6 ¾" (17 cm)
7 ¼" (18.6 cm)
7 ¼" (18.6 cm)

QUILT

7 ¼" (18.6 cm)
7 ¼" (18.6 cm)
29 ¼" (74.4 cm)
29 ¼" (74.4 cm)

a	b	c	d
e	f	g	h
i	j	k	l
m	n	o	p

CONSTRUCTION STEPS

For each block, sew the patchwork and appliqué pieces together to create the top (refer to the diagrams on pages 117-119 for individual block layouts). For blocks with embroidery, embroider as indicated on the template. Layer the top, batting, and backing. Quilt as indicated on the template. Use the binding strips to bind the block (refer to page 10). Embellish with lace or buttons as noted on the template. Connect the 16 blocks using ladder stitch (refer to page 11).

a

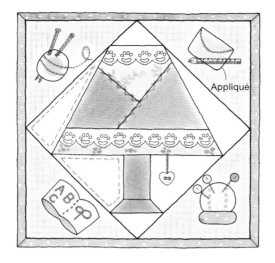

Appliqué

b

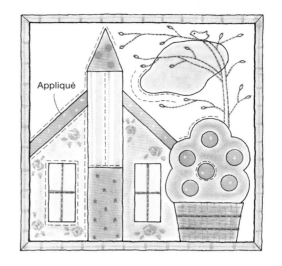

Appliqué

c Appliqué the handles

d Sew the borders

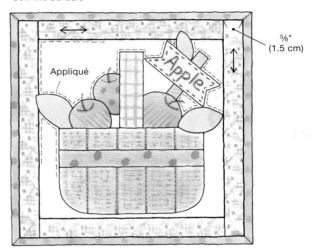

Appliqué

⅝"
(1.5 cm)

e

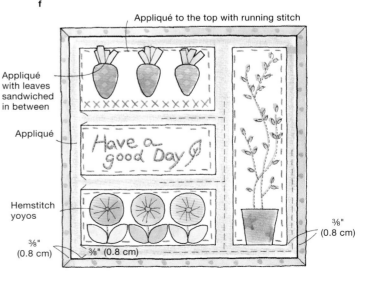

A

Appliqué

C

B

D

f

Appliqué to the top with running stitch

Appliqué
with leaves
sandwiched
in between

Appliqué

Have a
good Day

Hemstitch
yoyos

⅜"
(0.8 cm)

⅜" (0.8 cm)

⅜"
(0.8 cm)

g

Keep your life to the Sun

Appliqué

h Appliqué windows, door, and flag

i

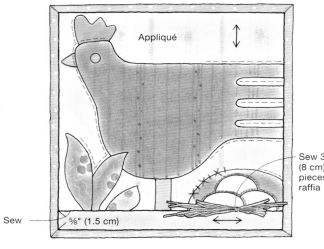

Appliqué

Sew 3 ⅛"
(8 cm) long
pieces of
raffia

Sew

⅝" (1.5 cm)

j

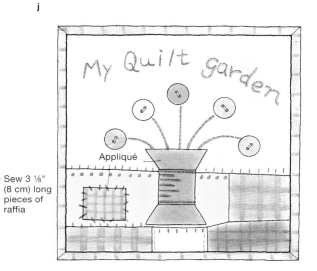

My Quilt garden

Appliqué

k Appliqué windows, door, leaves, and berries

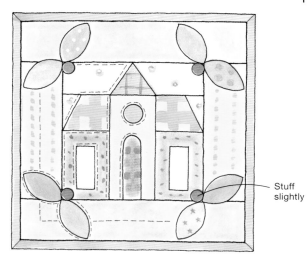

Stuff
slightly

l

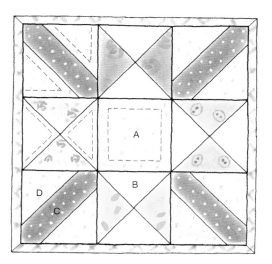

A

B

D

C

m   Insert flowers into calyx and hemstitch along the bottom only

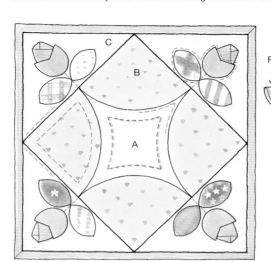

Fold flower

n   Make four of block B, then sew to A using inset seams

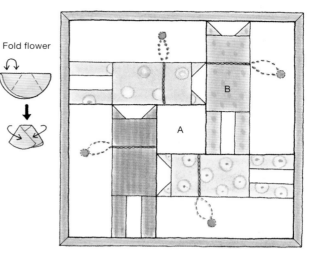

o

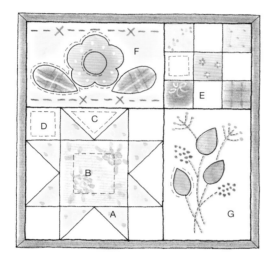

p   Appliqué flower and flower center

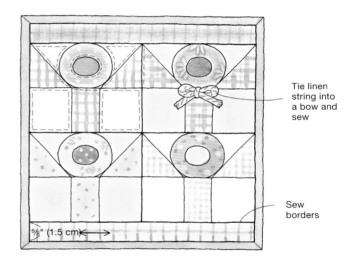

Tie linen string into a bow and sew

Sew borders

⅝" (1.5 cm)

Quilt Block Totes

MATERIALS

- **Patchwork and appliqué fabric:** Assorted scraps
- **Main fabric:** ⅝ yard of print fabric
- **Lining fabric:** ¾ yard of print fabric
- **Pocket binding fabric:** ¼ yard of print fabric
- **Batting:** 17 ¾" x 31 ½" (45 x 80 cm)
- One set of 20" (50 cm) handles
- No. 25 embroidery floss, lace, and buttons (as needed)

CUTTING INSTRUCTIONS

Trace and cut out your desired block template on Pattern Sheet A (refer to page 6 for instructions on using templates). Cut the following fabric pieces adding ¼" (0.7 cm) seam allowance:

- Patchwork pieces of assorted scraps
- Appliqué pieces of assorted scraps

Cut out the following pieces, which do not have templates, according to the measurements on the right (these measurements include seam allowance):

Main fabric:

- Top: 16 ¼" x 30 ½" (41.4 x 77.4 cm)
- Bag binding strips (cut lengthwise): 1 yard (1 m) of 1 ½" (3.5 cm) wide strips

Lining fabric:

- Lining: 17 ¼" x 30 ½" (44 x 77.4 cm)
- Pocket backing: 7 ¼" x 7 ¼" (18.4 x 18.4 cm)

Pocket binding fabric:

- Pocket binding strips (cut lengthwise): 31 ½" (80 cm) of 1 ½" (3.5 cm) wide strips

PATCHWORK DIAGRAM

Sew using ¼" (0.7 cm) seam allowance, unless otherwise noted.

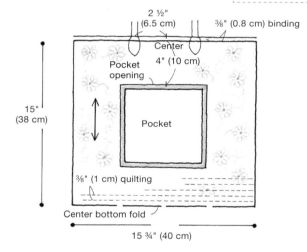

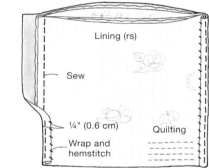

1.

CONSTRUCTION STEPS

1. Layer the bag top, batting, and lining. Quilt with horizontal lines about ⅜" (1 cm) apart. Fold the bag in half with right sides together. Use the technique shown on page 16 to sew the sides together and finish the seam allowance using the lining.

2. Make the desired block (refer to pages 116-119 for instructions). To make the pocket, hemstitch the block to the bag following the placement indicated in the above diagram. Use the strips to bind the bag opening. Backstitch the handles to the bag using two strands of quilting thread (refer to the above diagram for placement).

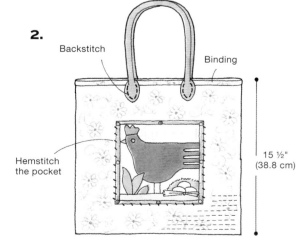

2.

① Hexagon Flower Tote

Instructions on page 15

- All templates are full-size.
- Trace or photocopy the templates. Do not cut this pattern sheet.
- Seam allowance is not included. Before cutting the fabric, add ¼" (0.7 cm) seam allowance to all pieces (unless otherwise noted).

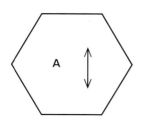

② City Life Tote

Instructions on page 18

Striped fabric   A   Text fabric

⑤ Two-Way Hexagon Purse

Instructions on page 31

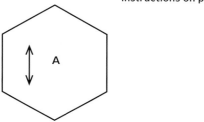

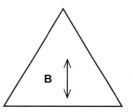

B

⑥ Cross-Body Bouquet Bag

Instructions on page 35

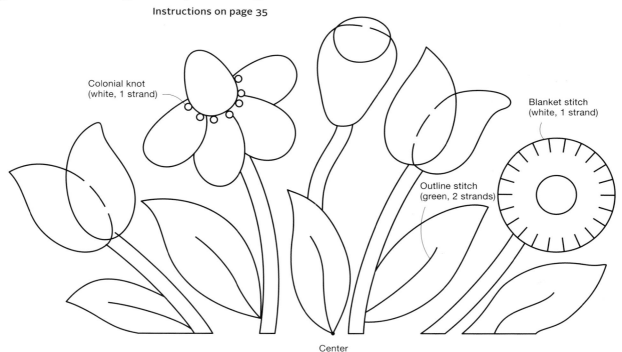

Colonial knot
(white, 1 strand)

Blanket stitch
(white, 1 strand)

Outline stitch
(green, 2 strands)

Center

Dancing Tulips Bucket Bag

Instructions on page 21

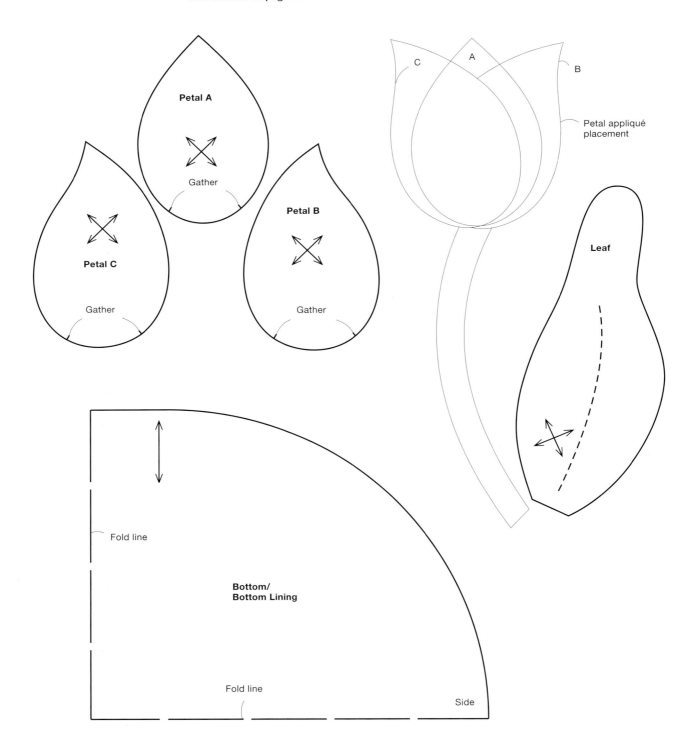

Petal A

Gather

Petal C

Gather

Petal B

Gather

C   A   B

Petal appliqué placement

Leaf

Fold line

Bottom/
Bottom Lining

Fold line

Side

④ Appliquéd Tulip Purse

Instructions on page 26

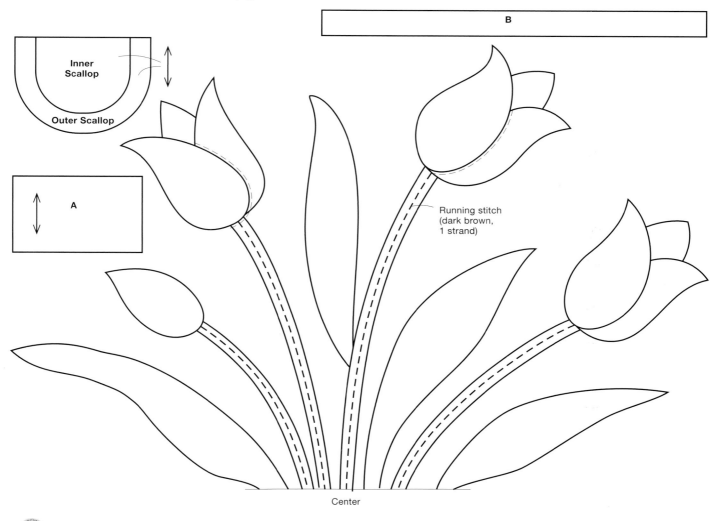

B

Inner Scallop

Outer Scallop

A

Running stitch (dark brown, 1 strand)

Center

⑦ Newsprint Backpack

Instructions on page 38

- All templates are full-size.
- Trace or photocopy the templates. Do not cut this pattern sheet.
- Seam allowance is not included. Before cutting the fabric, add ¼" (0.7 cm) seam allowance to all pieces (unless otherwise noted).

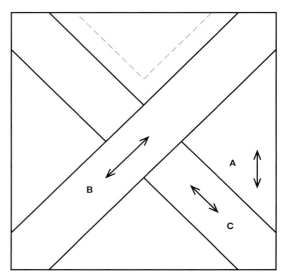

A

B

C

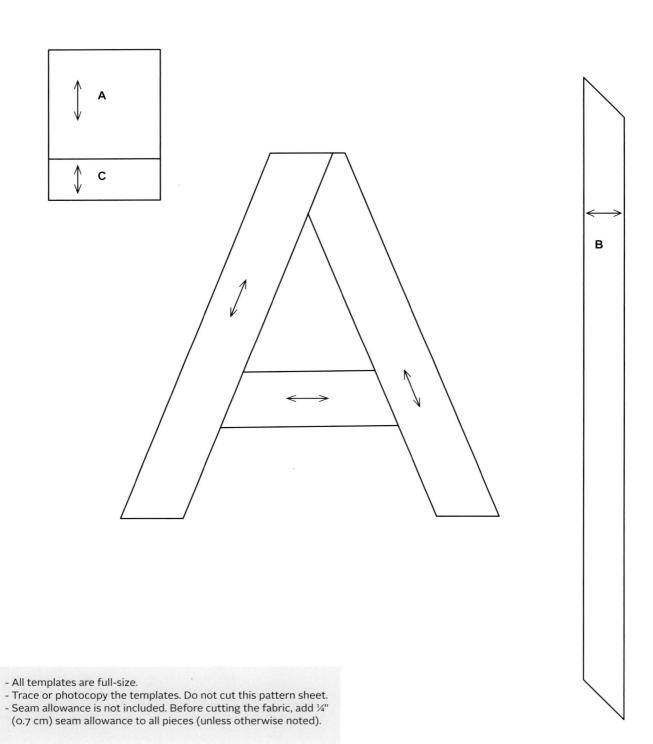

- All templates are full-size.
- Trace or photocopy the templates. Do not cut this pattern sheet.
- Seam allowance is not included. Before cutting the fabric, add ¼"
  (0.7 cm) seam allowance to all pieces (unless otherwise noted).

12 Irish Chain Tote

Instructions on page 55

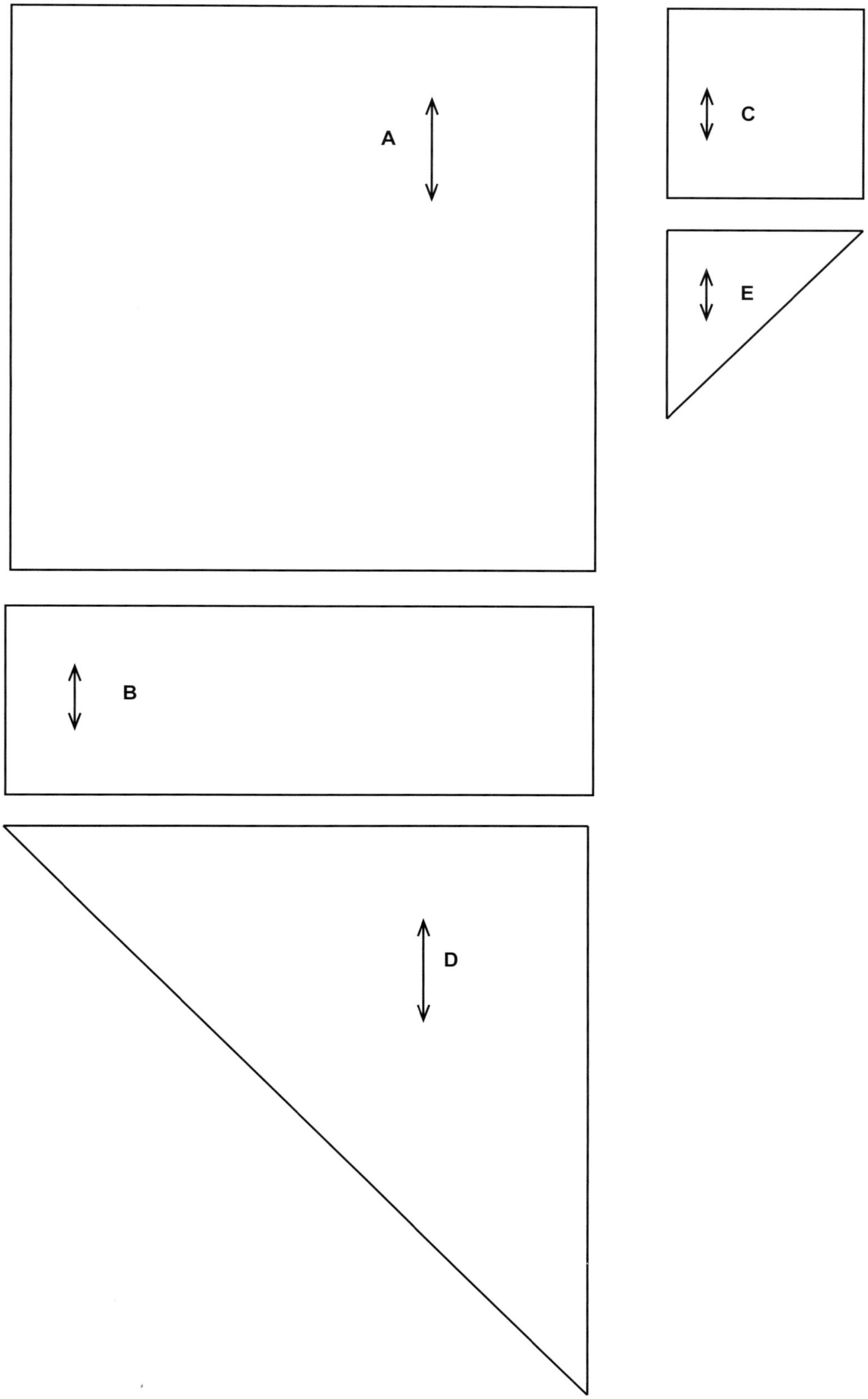

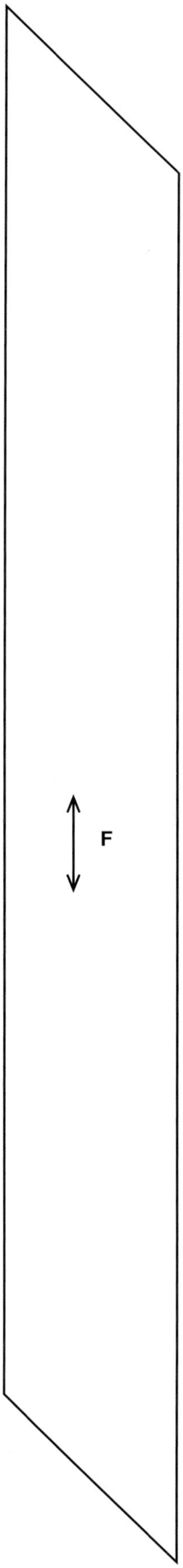

A

B

C

D

E

F

Embellished Patch Tote

Instructions on page 64

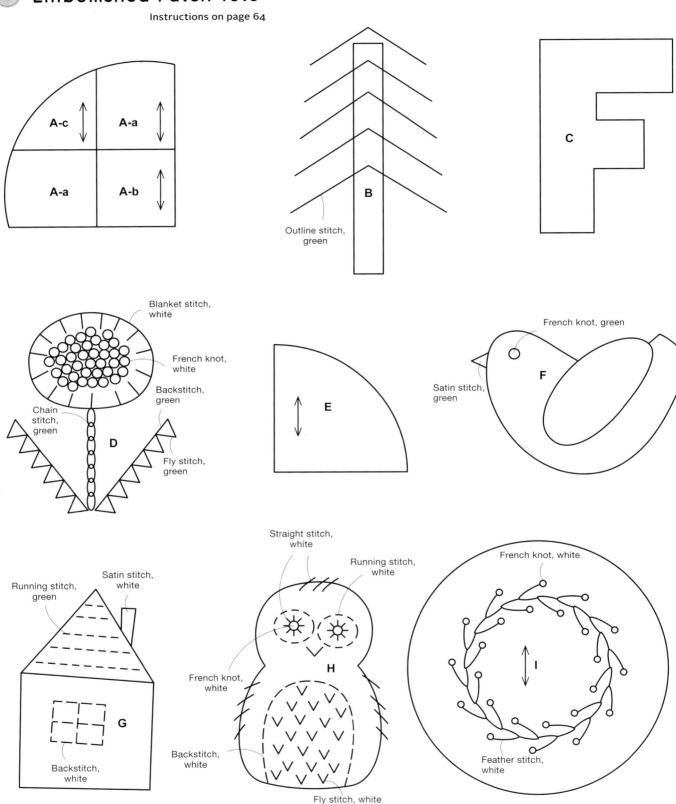

A-c A-a

A-a A-b

B

Outline stitch, green

C

Blanket stitch, white

French knot, white

Backstitch, green

Chain stitch, green

D

Fly stitch, green

E

French knot, green

F

Satin stitch, green

Running stitch, green

Satin stitch, white

G

Backstitch, white

Straight stitch, white

Running stitch, white

French knot, white

H

Backstitch, white

Fly stitch, white

French knot, white

I

Feather stitch, white

Appliquéd Boston Bag

Instructions on page 68

- All templates are full-size.
- Trace or photocopy the templates. Do not cut this pattern sheet.
- Seam allowance is not included. Before cutting the fabric, add ¼" (0.7 cm) seam allowance to all pieces (unless otherwise noted).

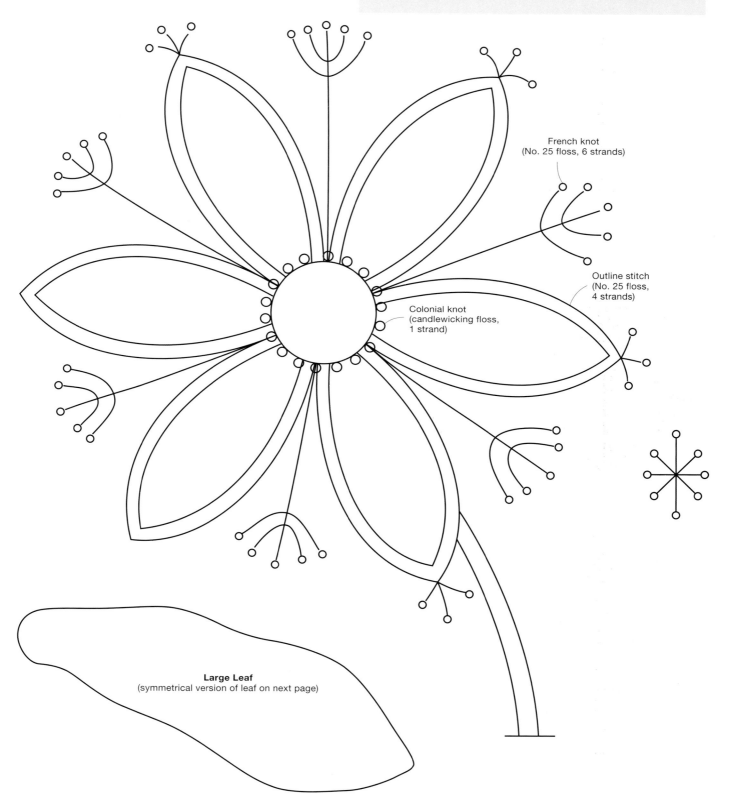

French knot
(No. 25 floss, 6 strands)

Outline stitch
(No. 25 floss,
4 strands)

Colonial knot
(candlewicking floss,
1 strand)

Large Leaf
(symmetrical version of leaf on next page)

- All templates are full-size.
- Trace or photocopy the templates. Do not cut this pattern sheet.
- Seam allowance is not included. Before cutting the fabric, add ¼"
  (0.7 cm) seam allowance to all pieces (unless otherwise noted).

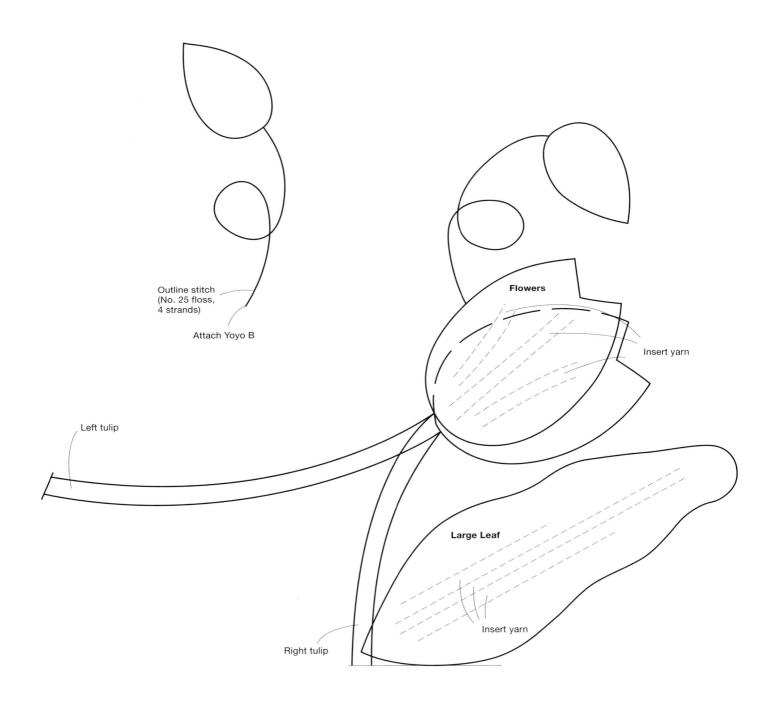

Outline stitch
(No. 25 floss,
4 strands)

Attach Yoyo B

Flowers

Insert yarn

Left tulip

Large Leaf

Insert yarn

Right tulip

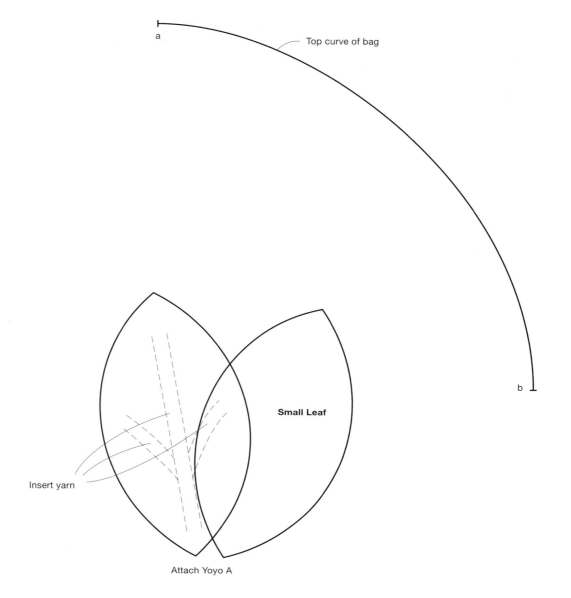

a

Top curve of bag

b

Small Leaf

Insert yarn

Attach Yoyo A

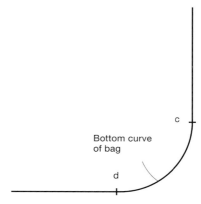

c

Bottom curve
of bag

d

Embroidered Eyeglass Case

Instructions on page 72

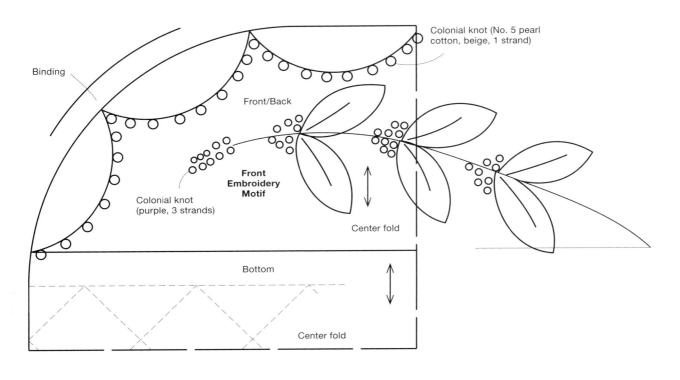

Binding

Colonial knot (No. 5 pearl cotton, beige, 1 strand)

Front/Back

Front Embroidery Motif

Colonial knot (purple, 3 strands)

Center fold

Bottom

Center fold

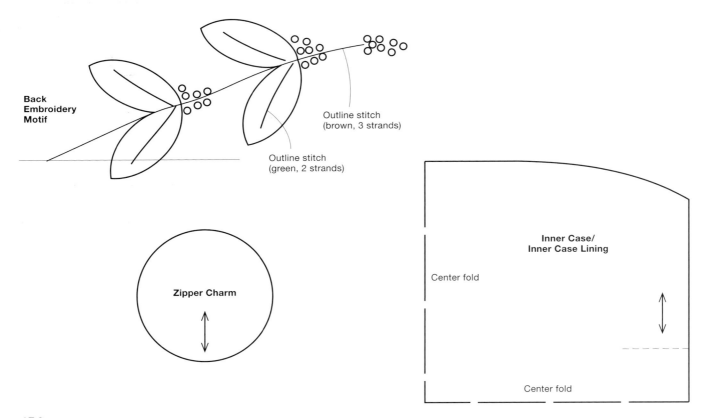

Back Embroidery Motif

Outline stitch (brown, 3 strands)

Outline stitch (green, 2 strands)

Zipper Charm

Inner Case/ Inner Case Lining

Center fold

Center fold

19 Village Tablet Case

Instructions on page 79

Instructions on page 79

- All templates are full-size.
- Trace or photocopy the templates. Do not cut this pattern sheet.
- Seam allowance is not included. Before cutting the fabric, add ¼" (0.7 cm) seam allowance to all pieces (unless otherwise noted).

Pocket

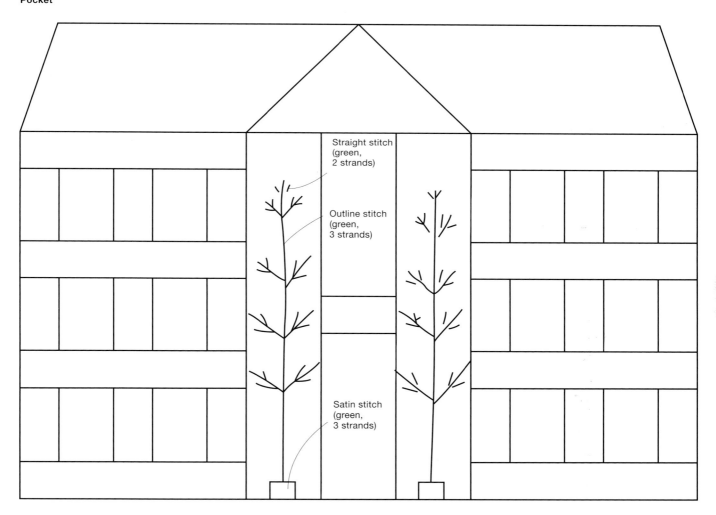

Straight stitch (green, 2 strands)

Outline stitch (green, 3 strands)

Satin stitch (green, 3 strands)

Align two stars when tracing templates ☆

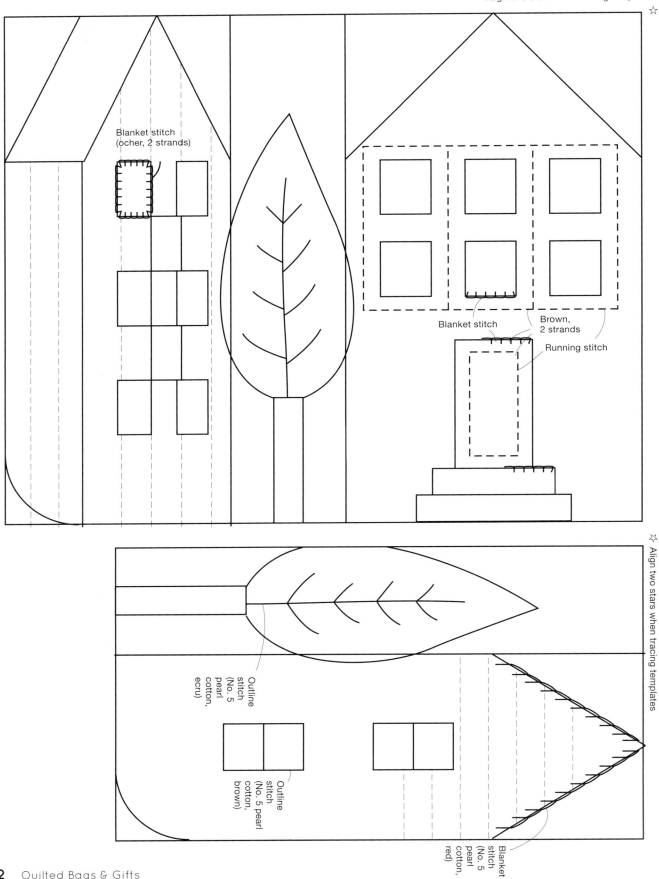

Blanket stitch
(ocher, 2 strands)

Blanket stitch

Brown,
2 strands

Running stitch

Outline
stitch
(No. 5
pearl
cotton,
ecru)

Outline
stitch
(No. 5 pearl
cotton,
brown)

Blanket
stitch
(No. 5
pearl
cotton,
red)

☆ Align two stars when tracing templates

20 # House Pencil Case

Instructions on page 83

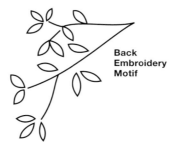

Back
Embroidery
Motif

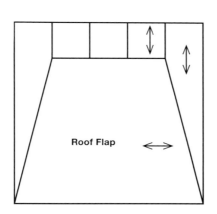

Roof Flap

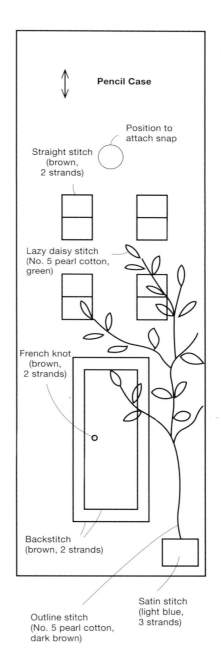

Pencil Case

Position to
attach snap

Straight stitch
(brown,
2 strands)

Lazy daisy stitch
(No. 5 pearl cotton,
green)

French knot
(brown,
2 strands)

Backstitch
(brown, 2 strands)

Outline stitch
(No. 5 pearl cotton,
dark brown)

Satin stitch
(light blue,
3 strands)

Bluebird Tea Mat

Instructions on page 87

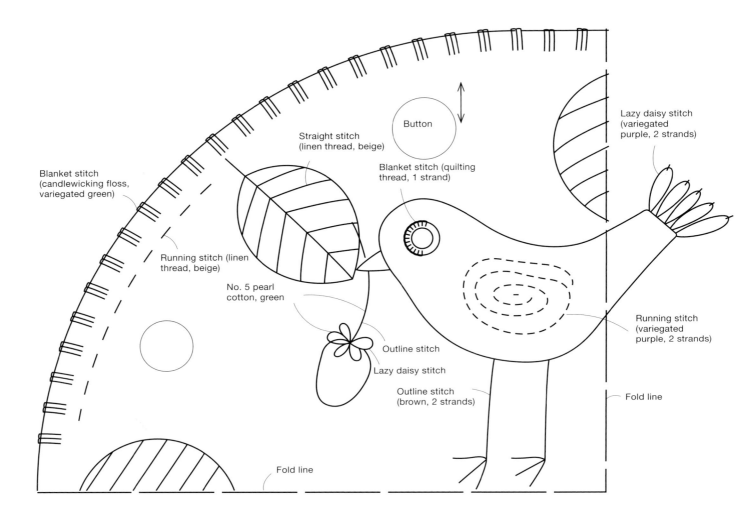

Blanket stitch
(candlewicking floss,
variegated green)

Running stitch (linen
thread, beige)

Straight stitch
(linen thread, beige)

Button

Blanket stitch (quilting
thread, 1 strand)

Lazy daisy stitch
(variegated
purple, 2 strands)

No. 5 pearl
cotton, green

Outline stitch

Lazy daisy stitch

Outline stitch
(brown, 2 strands)

Running stitch
(variegated
purple, 2 strands)

Fold line

Fold line

23 Hexagon Coin Purse

Instructions on page 89

- All templates are full-size.
- Trace or photocopy the templates. Do not cut this pattern sheet.
- Seam allowance is not included. Before cutting the fabric, add ¼" (0.7 cm) seam allowance to all pieces (unless otherwise noted).

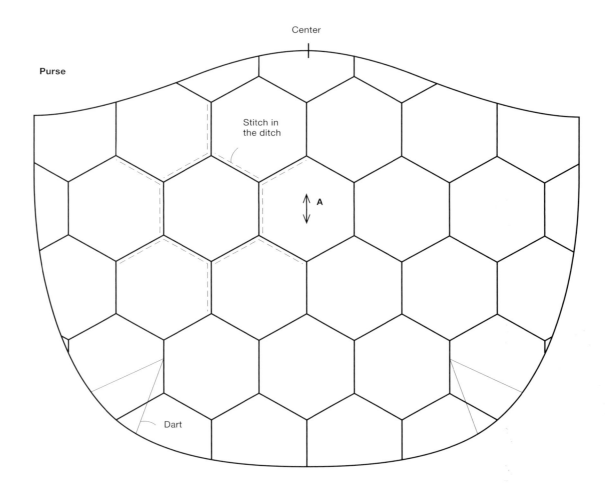

Center

Purse

Stitch in the ditch

A

Dart

24 Hexagon Zip Pouch

Instructions on 91

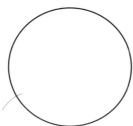

Covered button (do not add seam allowance)

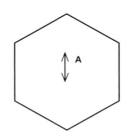

A

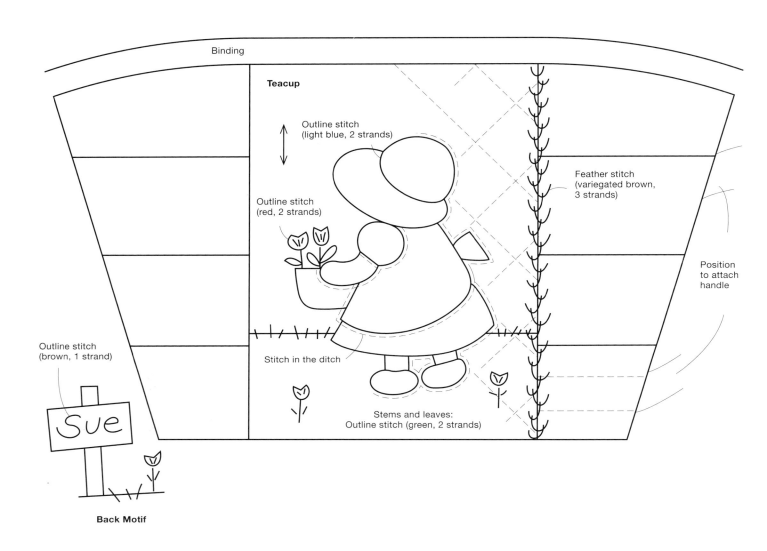

Binding

Teacup

Outline stitch
(light blue, 2 strands)

Outline stitch
(red, 2 strands)

Feather stitch
(variegated brown,
3 strands)

Position
to attach
handle

Outline stitch
(brown, 1 strand)

Stitch in the ditch

Stems and leaves:
Outline stitch (green, 2 strands)

Sue

Back Motif

Bottom

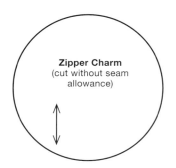

Zipper Charm
(cut without seam
allowance)

Owl Coin Purse

Instructions on page 96

- All templates are full-size.
- Trace or photocopy the templates. Do not cut this pattern sheet.
- Seam allowance is not included. Before cutting the fabric, add ¼" (0.7 cm) seam allowance to all pieces (unless otherwise noted).

☆ = Leave open to turn right side out

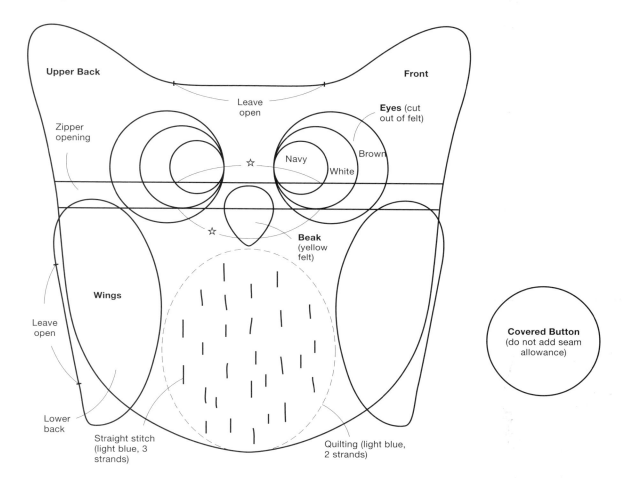

Binding

Colonial knot
(candlewicking floss)

Position to align
end of zipper

Button

Dark brown
(2 strands)

Cross-stitch

20 15

Outline stitch

Outline stitch
(brown, 2 strands)

Stitch in the
ditch

Lid/Bottom

Center fold line

Appliqué Border

Yoyo (do not add
seam allowance)

- All templates are full-size.
- Trace or photocopy the templates. Do not cut this pattern sheet.
- Seam allowance is not included. Before cutting the fabric, add ¼"
  (0.7 cm) seam allowance to all pieces (unless otherwise noted).

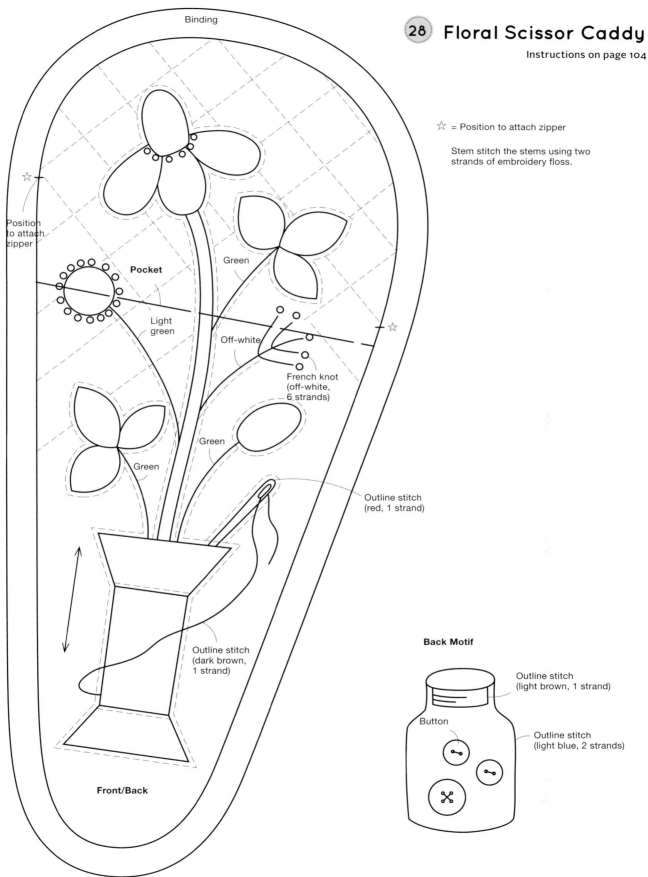

Binding

(28) Floral Scissor Caddy

Instructions on page 104

☆ = Position to attach zipper

Stem stitch the stems using two strands of embroidery floss.

Position to attach zipper

Pocket

Green

Light green

Off-white

French knot (off-white, 6 strands)

Green

Green

Outline stitch (red, 1 strand)

Outline stitch (dark brown, 1 strand)

Front/Back

Back Motif

Outline stitch (light brown, 1 strand)

Button

Outline stitch (light blue, 2 strands)

(29) Elephant Tape Measure Case

Instructions on page 106

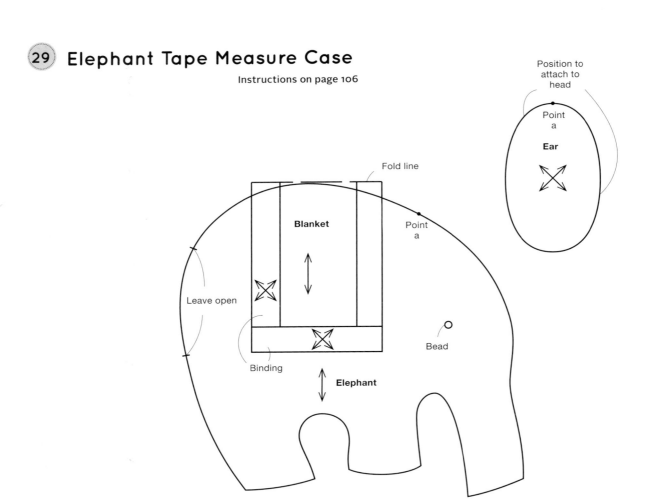

Position to attach to head

Point a

Ear

Fold line

Blanket

Point a

Leave open

Bead

Binding

Elephant

(30) Flower Pin Cushion

Instructions on page 107

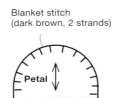

Blanket stitch
(dark brown, 2 strands)

Petal

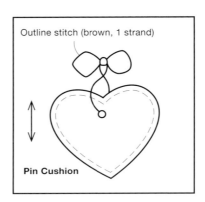

Outline stitch (brown, 1 strand)

Pin Cushion

(31) Floral Basket

(32) Floral Coasters

Instructions on pages 109 and 110

- All templates are full-size.
- Trace or photocopy the templates. Do not cut this pattern sheet.
- Seam allowance is not included. Before cutting the fabric, add ¼" (0.7 cm) seam allowance to all pieces (unless otherwise noted).

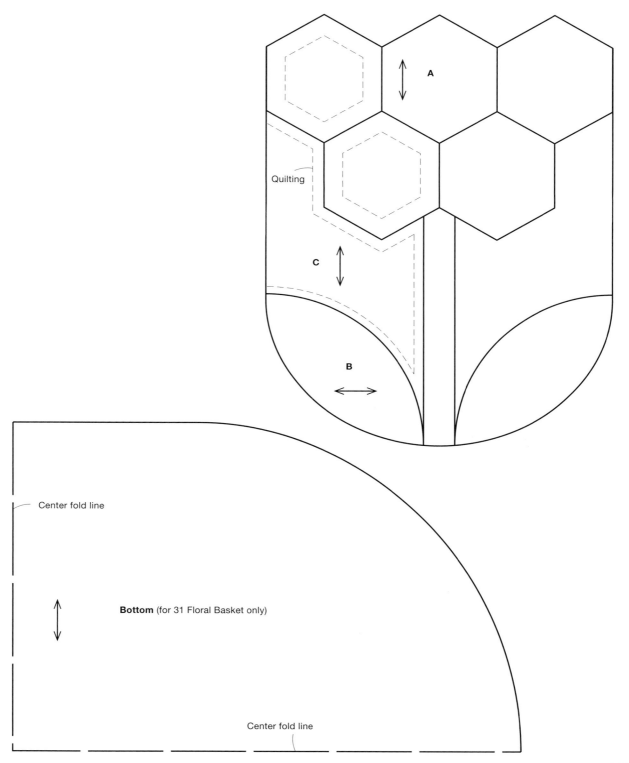

Quilting

A

C

B

Center fold line

Bottom (for 31 Floral Basket only)

Center fold line

33 Pastoral Wall Hanging

Instructions on page 112

Instructions on page 112

Align two stars when tracing templates ☆

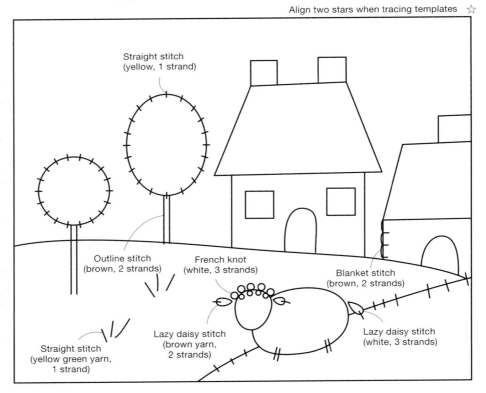

Straight stitch
(yellow, 1 strand)

Outline stitch
(brown, 2 strands)

French knot
(white, 3 strands)

Blanket stitch
(brown, 2 strands)

Lazy daisy stitch
(brown yarn,
2 strands)

Lazy daisy stitch
(white, 3 strands)

Straight stitch
(yellow green yarn,
1 strand)

☆ Align two stars when tracing templates

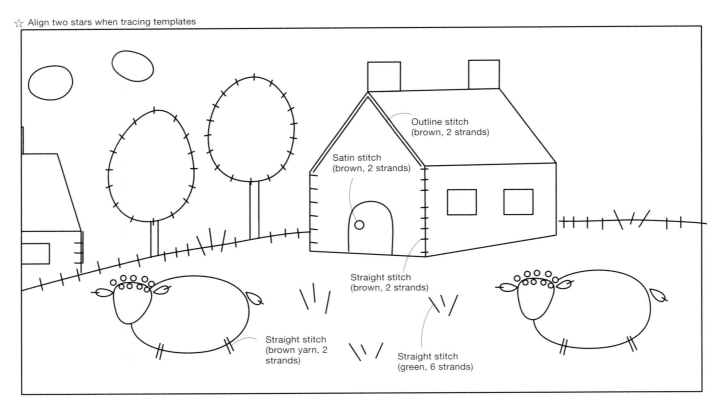

Outline stitch
(brown, 2 strands)

Satin stitch
(brown, 2 strands)

Straight stitch
(brown, 2 strands)

Straight stitch
(brown yarn, 2
strands)

Straight stitch
(green, 6 strands)

34 # Countryside Collage

Instructions on page 112

- All templates are full-size.
- Trace or photocopy the templates. Do not cut this pattern sheet.
- Seam allowance is not included. Before cutting the fabric, add ¼" (0.7 cm) seam allowance to all pieces (unless otherwise noted).

LOOKING FOR THE HARDWARE AND FABRICS USED IN THIS BOOK?

Check out the following international resources:

VAZZ HOUSE

www.vazz.co.jp

Akemi Shibata's online store, offering kits, fabric, and hardware. Ships from Japan.

ZAKKA WORKSHOP

www.zakkaworkshop.com

Publisher site offering select hardware for some of the popular projects in the book. Ships from the United States.

ETSY

www.etsy.com

Many great Etsy shops offer a range of taupe and colorful print fabric, bag hardware, and notions perfect for making the projects in this book. Ships from sellers based around the world.

U-HANDBAG

www.u-handbag.com

Offers a wide selection of handles, hardware, and other bag-making supplies. Ships from the United Kingdom.

Akemi Shibata's yarn-dyed fabric line is produced by Lecien Fabrics of Japan. Ask your local quilt shop about Lecien fabrics.